Effective Nonprofit Board Governance

Roles, Responsibilities, and Best Practices for Committees and Directors

Matthew B. Scraper

Disclaimers and Copyright Information

ISBN 978-1-300-75998-0
Imprint: Lulu.com

Copyright Information

For permission requests, please contact the author through **MBS Operations** at **matthew@mbsoperations.com**.

Publisher Information

Published by Lulu Press, Inc.
For more information, visit **www.lulu.com**.

Disclaimer

The information provided in this book is based on the author's personal experiences, research, and professional expertise. While every effort has been made to ensure accuracy and relevance, this book is not intended as legal, financial, or professional advice. Readers are encouraged to seek appropriate counsel for their specific circumstances.

Acknowledgments

The author has made every effort to acknowledge and credit all sources and references used in this book. Any omissions or errors are unintentional and will be corrected in future editions, if notified.

Trademarks

All trademarks, service marks, product names, or named features mentioned in this book are the property of their respective owners. Use of these names does not imply any affiliation or endorsement.

Contact Information

For inquiries, permissions, or additional resources, visit **www.mbsoperations.com**.

First Edition

Printed in the United States of America.

Table of Contents

Contents

Table of Contents 4

Introduction 6

Chapter 1: Understanding the Role of the Board of Directors 10

Chapter 2: The Board Governance Committee 28

Chapter 3: The Finance Committee 41

Chapter 4: The Audit Committee 57

Chapter 5: The Development Committee 77

Chapter 6: The Program(s) Committee 88

Chapter 7: The Executive Committee 100

Chapter 8: Board Tools, Technology, and Resources 111

Chapter 9: Conclusion 118

Appendix: Board Bylaws Template and Committee Charter Templates 123

   1. Board Bylaws Template 123

   2. Committee Charter Templates 127

      Governance Committee Charter 127

      Finance Committee Charter 128

      Audit Committee Charter 129

Development Committee Charter 130

Program Committee Charter 131

Executive Committee Charter 132

Recommended Reading 133

Introduction

Purpose of the Book

The purpose of this book is to provide a comprehensive guide to nonprofit board governance, offering clear, actionable insights for board members, executive leadership, and staff. It addresses the essential roles and responsibilities of the board of directors and its key committees, equipping nonprofit leaders with the tools they need to strengthen governance, increase accountability, and drive organizational success. This book serves as both a practical reference and a training resource for nonprofit boards at every stage of development.

Importance of Board Governance in Nonprofits

Effective board governance is crucial to the success of any nonprofit organization. Strong governance ensures legal and ethical integrity, financial accountability, and mission alignment. Boards play a vital role in strategic oversight, executive leadership support, and organizational risk management. When board members understand their roles and responsibilities, nonprofits can achieve greater transparency, sustainability, and impact. This book emphasizes the importance of governance best practices that empower boards to be proactive, engaged, and mission-driven.

Overview of Board Committees and Their Roles

Nonprofit boards typically operate through a series of committees, each with a distinct focus and set of responsibilities. These committees enable the board to function more efficiently and make informed decisions. This book explores the following key committees in detail:

- **Board Governance Committee**: Manages board member recruitment, onboarding, and evaluation.

- **Finance Committee**: Provides oversight of the organization's financial health, budget, and reporting.

- **Audit Committee**: Engages with external auditors, ensures financial transparency, and assesses internal controls.

- **Development Committee**: Supports fundraising strategy and donor engagement efforts.

- **Program(s) Committee**: Monitors programmatic impact, alignment with mission, and strategic objectives.

- **Executive Committee**: Acts on behalf of the board between full board meetings and handles urgent matters.

Each chapter of this book focuses on a specific committee, outlining its role, structure, and best practices for effective governance. By understanding the purpose and responsibilities of each committee, nonprofit leaders can ensure their board operates with clarity and efficiency.

How to Use This Book (for Board Members, Staff, and Executive Leadership)

This book is designed to be a practical, user-friendly resource for various stakeholders involved in nonprofit governance. Here's how different audiences can benefit:

- **Board Members**: Use this book to understand your role, enhance your participation, and strengthen your impact. The guidance provided will help you navigate committee responsibilities, participate in board activities, and engage in strategic decision-making.

- **Executive Leadership**: As an executive director, CEO, or senior leader, this book will provide insights into how to best support the board, collaborate with committee chairs, and facilitate effective governance practices. It will also help you understand the appropriate role of staff in supporting board activities.

- **Staff and Board Liaisons**: Staff members who support board committees can use this book to clarify their roles, expectations, and responsibilities. It offers practical tools, such as sample templates, annual timelines, and checklists, that make it easier for staff to provide effective support to board committees.

By following the guidance in this book, board members, executive leaders, and staff will be equipped with the knowledge, skills, and tools they need to build a highly effective and mission-driven governance structure. This guidance is deeply personal to me as the author. My journey in nonprofit leadership spans over two decades, during which I've served as Chief Operating Officer for multiple nonprofit organizations. I've had the privilege of working alongside dedicated board members and executive leaders to develop governance systems, lead board committees, and navigate complex transitions in executive leadership. Through these experiences, I've seen firsthand the impact that strong governance can have on mission-driven work. My approach is shaped not just by theory, but by real-world application, and I'm committed to sharing practical, actionable advice to empower every reader of this book.

Chapter 1: Understanding the Role of the Board of Directors

Purpose and Responsibilities of the Board of Directors

The Board of Directors plays a fundamental role in nonprofit governance. Its core responsibilities include providing strategic direction, oversight, and accountability to ensure the organization's mission is fulfilled. Board members act as stewards of the nonprofit's resources, ensuring legal and ethical compliance, financial stability, and operational integrity.

Fiduciary Duties

1. **Duty of Care**: Board members must act with the level of care, diligence, and competence that an ordinarily prudent person would exercise in similar circumstances. This means actively participating in meetings, reviewing materials in advance, and making informed decisions in the best interest of the organization.

2. **Duty of Loyalty**: Board members must prioritize the interests of the nonprofit above their own personal or professional interests. This requires avoiding conflicts of interest and disclosing any potential conflicts to the board.

3. **Duty of Obedience**: Board members must ensure the nonprofit's activities remain aligned with its

mission and comply with applicable laws, regulations, and internal governing documents. This duty reinforces accountability to donors, beneficiaries, and the public.

Oversight vs. Management: Clarifying Boundaries

The board's role is to provide oversight, not to manage the day-to-day operations of the nonprofit. This distinction is critical for maintaining an effective partnership between the board and executive leadership. Oversight responsibilities include approving strategy, monitoring financial health, and evaluating the executive director's performance. Management tasks, such as staff supervision, program execution, and daily operations, are the responsibility of the executive director and staff.

To understand this distinction more clearly, it's important to differentiate between strategy and tactics. **Strategy** refers to the high-level plan designed to achieve long-term organizational goals. It focuses on "what" the organization aims to accomplish and "why" those objectives are essential. Board members are responsible for shaping and approving the overall strategy, ensuring that it aligns with the mission and long-term vision of the nonprofit. On the other hand, **tactics** are the specific actions and methods used to implement the strategy. Tactics answer the "how" questions—how will we achieve these goals? Tactics are developed and executed by the executive director and staff. By maintaining this separation of responsibilities, the board can focus on strategic oversight while allowing staff to focus on operational execution.

Key Roles within the Board

A nonprofit board is thoughtfully composed to ensure effective governance and support key leadership functions. Each role within the board is distinct yet interconnected, with every member playing a vital part in advancing the organization's mission. The structure is intentionally designed to promote collaboration, accountability, and strategic alignment. By leveraging the unique strengths of each role, the board can make well-informed decisions, provide oversight, and ensure the nonprofit remains focused on its mission-driven goals.

- **Chair/President**: The Chair is the primary leader of the board, facilitating meetings, guiding strategic discussions, and serving as the main liaison with the executive director. The Chair ensures meetings remain focused and productive, while also providing key support during leadership transitions.

- **Vice Chair**: The Vice Chair supports the Chair and steps in to fulfill the Chair's role when needed. This role is often seen as a natural successor to the Chair role in future board terms.

- **Secretary**: Responsible for documenting board activities, recording meeting minutes, and maintaining essential governance records. The Secretary's role is crucial for maintaining institutional knowledge and ensuring legal compliance.

- **Treasurer**: The financial steward of the board, the Treasurer oversees the organization's financial health, budget, and audits. This role works closely with the executive director and finance staff to ensure transparent and accurate financial reporting.

- **General Board Members**: Board members without officer roles contribute to decision-making, participate in committee work, and support fundraising, advocacy, and mission-driven activities. Each member brings unique perspectives and skills that strengthen the board's collective capacity.

Role of Board Members vs. Role of the Executive Director/CEO

The board governs; the executive director manages. While board members focus on strategy, oversight, and policy, the executive director handles operational management and staff leadership. The executive director provides updates, offers recommendations, and ensures the board has the information it needs to make sound decisions.

When selecting the title of the organization's leader, it's important to consider the messaging and perception that comes with each option. The title **Executive Director** is often associated with nonprofit organizations and emphasizes the operational and administrative role of the position. It reflects the leader's primary responsibility to execute the strategy set by the board. In contrast, the title **Chief Executive Officer (CEO)** is more commonly associated with corporate structures and conveys a sense of strategic leadership and organizational authority. Some nonprofits choose to use "CEO" to signal the organization's complexity, prominence, or growth stage. Selecting between "Executive Director" and "CEO" depends on how the organization wants to position itself to donors, funders, and external stakeholders. It's also possible for an organization to use both titles simultaneously, such as "Executive Director & CEO," to convey both roles' strategic and operational elements.

Board Composition and Recruitment

A high-functioning board requires the right mix of skills, experience, and perspectives to support the nonprofit's mission. This mix allows the board to provide thoughtful oversight, informed decision-making, and strategic guidance. Intentional recruitment is critical to achieving this balance, ensuring that each member brings unique value to the boardroom. This process involves identifying specific skills gaps, seeking individuals with diverse lived experiences, and fostering an inclusive environment where different perspectives are respected and valued. By prioritizing strategic recruitment, nonprofits can build a board that is dynamic, adaptable, and equipped to address the challenges and opportunities facing the organization.

Identifying Skills, Expertise, and Diversity Needs

Boards should actively seek members with skills in areas such as finance, legal, fundraising, marketing, human resources, and nonprofit management. Equally important is ensuring diversity in race, gender, age, lived experiences, and professional backgrounds to promote equitable decision-making and better represent the community served by the organization.

Use of a Board Recruitment Matrix

A board recruitment matrix is a tool that visually maps the board's current skills and demographics. This matrix highlights gaps in representation and expertise, helping the board prioritize recruitment efforts to build a more well-rounded team. This process ensures thoughtful and strategic board member selection.

Example of a Board Recruitment Matrix:

Name	Professional Skills	Diversity	Community Representation	Term Expiration	Gaps to Address
Jane Doe	Legal, Compliance	Female, Latinx	Community Health	June 2025	None
John Smith	Finance, Accounting	Male, White	Corporate Partnerships	December 2024	Digital Marketing
Amara Johnson	Fundraising, Events	Female, Black	Faith-Based Organizations	March 2026	Technology/IT
Carlos Reyes	Technology, IT	Male, Latinx	Education Sector	September 2025	Marketing Expertise
Priya Patel	Marketing, Branding	Female, South Asian	Youth Advocacy	November 2023	Legal Expertise

This matrix identifies the skills and demographics represented on the current board, providing a clear visual

15

of where gaps exist. By reviewing the "Gaps to Address" column, the governance committee can prioritize recruitment for the specific skills and perspectives needed to create a well-rounded and effective board.

Annual Timeline of Board Responsibilities

Effective boards operate on an annual schedule that addresses key governance activities. This structured approach ensures that board members are prepared for critical deadlines and major decision points throughout the year. By structuring responsibilities into a clear timeline, the board can prioritize essential tasks like budget approvals, performance evaluations, and strategic planning. This proactive approach allows the board to focus on long-term goals while maintaining oversight of immediate operational needs.

An annual schedule typically includes quarterly milestones that align with the organization's fiscal year and reporting obligations. For example, in the first quarter, the board may focus on reviewing the fiscal year's budget, setting strategic priorities, and orienting new board members. In the second quarter, efforts may shift to mid-year strategy reviews, progress reports on annual goals, and financial performance analysis. The third quarter often involves preparing for leadership transitions, conducting board member self-assessments, and initiating the executive director's evaluation process. The fourth quarter is often dedicated to finalizing the next fiscal year's budget, electing new officers, and reflecting on the organization's overall impact.

By following this structured timeline, the board can avoid reactive decision-making and maintain a steady rhythm of governance. This approach also ensures that board members remain engaged and fully aware of their responsibilities throughout the year, fostering a culture of accountability and strategic focus.

Key Responsibilities by Quarter

- **Quarter 1 (July - September):** Approve the fiscal year budget, review strategic goals, set board member expectations, and conduct an initial board orientation for new members.

- **Quarter 2 (October - December):** Host a mid-year strategic review, prepare for board recruitment, and review financial performance against the approved budget.

- **Quarter 3 (January - March):** Conduct annual board self-assessments, begin executive director evaluations, and plan for upcoming board leadership transitions.

- **Quarter 4 (April - June):** Finalize the budget for the next fiscal year, complete executive director performance reviews, and elect new board officers.

Board Retreats, Strategic Planning, and Annual Reviews

Annual board retreats provide an opportunity to focus on long-term strategy, assess the board's effectiveness, and strengthen team cohesion. These retreats are typically held offsite to allow for uninterrupted time dedicated to reflection, planning, and open dialogue. Key components of a successful board retreat include:

- **Strategic Planning Sessions**: Facilitated discussions aimed at reviewing the organization's mission, vision, and strategic priorities. This process often involves a SWOT analysis (Strengths, Weaknesses, Opportunities, and Threats) and goal-setting for the upcoming year.

- **Board Development and Training**: Sessions that educate board members on their roles, fiduciary responsibilities, and key governance topics. This component is especially useful for new board members or as a refresher for seasoned members.

- **Team Building Activities**: Activities designed to strengthen relationships among board members and foster a sense of shared commitment to the organization's mission.

- **Executive Director Check-in and Feedback**: A dedicated session for board members to engage in candid dialogue with the executive director, discussing performance, organizational challenges, and leadership support needs.

Strategic planning is an essential aspect of a board's governance role. The process should be inclusive and collaborative, involving board members, executive leadership, and key stakeholders. Effective strategic planning includes the following steps:

18

1. **Pre-Planning and Preparation**: This involves gathering data, identifying key issues, and securing facilitator support if needed. Board members should review prior strategic plans, organizational reports, and relevant market or industry trends.

2. **Vision and Mission Alignment**: During the retreat, board members review the organization's mission and vision to ensure alignment with current and future goals.

3. **Goal Setting and Prioritization**: Board members identify key objectives for the coming year and beyond. This process often involves breaking down broad goals into actionable steps and assigning responsibility for each task.

4. **Resource Assessment and Capacity Review**: The board reviews financial, human, and operational resources to ensure that goals are realistic and achievable.

5. **Implementation Plan Development**: Clear timelines, benchmarks, and accountability measures are established to track progress on strategic goals throughout the year.

Annual reviews include evaluating board member performance, conducting executive director evaluations, and reviewing the organization's overall impact. These reviews allow the board to assess its effectiveness, ensure accountability, and make necessary adjustments for future success.

Meeting Best Practices

Board meetings are essential to effective governance. They provide the platform for discussion, decision-making, and oversight. To maximize impact, meetings should be efficient, well-structured, and mission-focused.

Frequency, Format, and Facilitation Guidelines

Boards typically meet quarterly, with some meeting more frequently depending on organizational needs. Meetings can be in-person, virtual, or hybrid, depending on member availability and location. Effective facilitation ensures meetings remain on track and allows for all voices to be heard.

Effective Agenda Setting and Consent Agendas

A clear agenda, shared in advance, sets expectations for the meeting's purpose and goals. Consent agendas are used to streamline routine items like meeting minutes, freeing up time for strategic discussion.

Example of a Board Meeting Agenda

Board of Directors Meeting Agenda
Date: [Insert Date]
Time: [Insert Time]
Location: [Insert Location or Virtual Link]

1. **Welcome and Call to Order** (5 minutes)

    o   Chair's welcome and meeting overview

    o   Roll call and introductions

2. **Consent Agenda** (10 minutes)

   o   Approval of previous meeting minutes

   o   Review of routine reports (e.g., financial reports, committee reports)

3. **Executive Director's Report** (15 minutes)

   o   Update on key organizational activities

   o   Discussion of key challenges and opportunities

4. **Finance Report** (20 minutes)

   o   Presentation of financial statements

   o   Review of budget variances

   o   Discussion of any required board actions related to finances

5. **Committee Reports** (15 minutes)

   o   Updates from standing and ad hoc committees (e.g., Governance, Development, Audit)

   o   Recommendations for board actions or approvals

6. **Strategic Discussion/Key Issues** (30 minutes)

   o   Discussion of major strategic initiatives or issues

   o   Breakout groups (if applicable)

- Collection of key takeaways and action items

7. **Action Items and Decisions** (10 minutes)

   - Recap of decisions made during the meeting

   - Confirmation of follow-up actions, deadlines, and accountability

8. **New Business and Open Floor** (10 minutes)

   - Opportunity for board members to raise additional items

9. **Executive Session (if applicable)** (10-15 minutes)

   - Discussion without staff present (if necessary)

10. **Adjournment**

- Chair closes the meeting and confirms next meeting date

This agenda format ensures that meetings are well-structured, focused on strategic priorities, and respectful of board members' time. The use of a consent agenda streamlines routine approvals, leaving more time for in-depth discussions and decision-making on mission-critical issues.

What is a Consent Agenda? A consent agenda is a tool used to streamline the approval process for routine, non-controversial items that do not require discussion. Instead of reviewing each item individually, all items in the consent agenda are approved in one collective vote. This approach allows the board to save valuable time and focus on more critical agenda items.

What Items Typically Appear on a Consent Agenda? Items included in a consent agenda often have straightforward approvals or are recurring in nature. Examples include:

- Approval of previous meeting minutes

- Routine committee reports (Governance, Finance, Development, etc.)

- Staff updates that do not require action

- Standard policy updates or procedural changes

How Does a Consent Agenda Work?

1. **Pre-Meeting Preparation**: The board chair and executive director collaborate to identify which items belong on the consent agenda. Supporting documents for each item are sent to board members in advance of the meeting.

2. **Review by Board Members**: Board members review the consent agenda and related materials prior to the meeting. If any member believes an item needs further discussion, they can request its removal from the consent agenda.

3. **Approval During the Meeting**: At the meeting, the chair calls for a motion to approve the consent agenda. Once moved and seconded, the board

votes on all items in the consent agenda as a single action.

4. **Removal of Items**: If a board member requests the removal of an item, it is moved to the main agenda for further discussion.

Benefits of a Consent Agenda

- **Time-Saving**: Streamlines routine approvals, allowing more time for strategic discussions.

- **Focus on Priorities**: Frees up meeting time for critical decision-making.

- **Encourages Preparation**: Board members must review consent agenda materials in advance, promoting accountability and engagement.

By incorporating a consent agenda, nonprofit boards can run more efficient, purposeful meetings, ensuring that time is spent where it matters most.

Use of Board Portals and Document Storage

Board portals (online platforms) provide centralized access to key documents, such as meeting agendas, financial reports, and governance materials. Secure document storage ensures confidentiality and promotes transparency for board members.

Staff Liaison Roles and Responsibilities

While the board's role is governance, staff play a key support role that is essential to the board's effectiveness.

Staff liaisons act as a bridge between the board and the organization's operational activities, ensuring clear communication, timely preparation of materials, and follow-through on board decisions. They provide administrative support, schedule meetings, and distribute key documents like board packets, agendas, and financial reports. Staff liaisons also play a critical role in onboarding new board members, facilitating introductions, and providing necessary orientation materials. Their role is vital to maintaining an organized, well-informed, and engaged board that can focus on strategic oversight rather than operational details. Effective staff liaisons anticipate board needs, prepare executive summaries for complex issues, and ensure follow-up actions are clearly assigned and tracked.

Staff Support for Board Activities

Staff support enables board members to focus on strategic oversight rather than operational details. Common support activities include preparing reports, managing logistics, and facilitating communication.

Key Staff Positions to Support the Board

- **Executive Director/CEO**: Serves as the primary staff liaison, offering regular updates and recommendations to the board.

- **Chief Operating Officer (COO)**: Oversees daily operations and ensures the alignment of operational activities with strategic goals. The COO provides operational insights to the board, supports the implementation of board directives, and serves as a liaison for committees that require input on operational matters, such as finance, governance, or facilities.

- **Chief Financial Officer (CFO) or Finance Director**: Provides financial reports, budget updates, and audit support to the board and finance committee.

- **Board Liaison or Governance Specialist**: Manages logistics for board meetings, supports board recruitment, and maintains governance records.

As we conclude this chapter, it's clear that effective board governance is the foundation of a successful nonprofit organization. The roles, responsibilities, and practices outlined here serve as a blueprint for creating a governance structure that is both strategic and mission-driven. By understanding key concepts like fiduciary duties, oversight versus management, and the distinct roles of board members and executive leadership, nonprofits can establish a clear path toward accountability, impact, and sustainability.

Every board member, whether they serve as Chair, Treasurer, or a general member, plays a vital role in shaping the future of the organization. The thoughtful recruitment of diverse and skilled board members ensures that the organization benefits from a range of perspectives, while tools like the board recruitment matrix bring transparency and strategy to the selection process. By structuring their work around an annual timeline, boards can remain proactive rather than reactive, ensuring that key responsibilities like budget approval, strategic planning, and executive evaluations are addressed on time.

This chapter has also highlighted the importance of board retreats and the role of strategic planning. These moments of reflection, alignment, and forward-thinking allow boards to recalibrate and set bold goals for the future. The inclusion of meeting best practices, consent agendas, and the role of staff liaisons further supports a governance model that is efficient, collaborative, and mission-focused.

With a well-structured board, a clear understanding of responsibilities, and a commitment to continuous learning, nonprofits can position themselves to meet challenges head-on and seize new opportunities for growth and impact. As you move forward, remember that governance is not a one-time event—it's an ongoing process of learning, refining, and growing. The principles outlined in this chapter serve as a guide, but it's the commitment and intentionality of board members, staff, and executive leadership that truly drive a nonprofit's success.

Chapter 2: The Board Governance Committee

Role and Purpose of the Governance Committee

The Governance Committee serves as the architect of the board's structure, membership, and overall effectiveness. This committee ensures that the board is composed of the right people with the right skills, experiences, and perspectives to advance the organization's mission. Acting as the "board of the board," the Governance Committee is responsible for overseeing key governance functions that support the board's growth, accountability, and sustainability.

One of the committee's most critical roles is to maintain a balanced and effective board composition. This involves identifying gaps in skills, expertise, and demographic representation that are needed to achieve the organization's strategic goals. By utilizing a Board Recruitment Matrix, the committee can visualize the current board's strengths and identify areas where new perspectives or competencies are required. This information is then used to develop a targeted recruitment strategy.

Once potential board members are identified, the Governance Committee facilitates the recruitment process, which may include candidate outreach, interviews, and formal recommendations to the full board.

Upon a new member's approval, the committee oversees onboarding, ensuring new members receive orientation materials, introductions to staff, and training on governance best practices. This comprehensive onboarding process empowers new board members to contribute effectively from the outset.

The Governance Committee also supports ongoing board development through periodic evaluations. These evaluations may include board self-assessments and performance reviews for individual members. The feedback gathered from these assessments informs future training, role adjustments, and succession planning for key board positions such as Chair, Vice Chair, Secretary, and Treasurer. By fostering an environment of continuous improvement, the Governance Committee ensures that the board remains dynamic, engaged, and strategically aligned with the organization's mission.

Oversight of Board Composition and Structure

The Governance Committee plays a vital role in shaping the overall composition and structure of the board. Its primary responsibility is to ensure that the board reflects the skills, experiences, and diversity required to effectively guide the organization. This process begins with a comprehensive analysis of the board's existing strengths and areas for growth. Using a board recruitment matrix, the committee identifies gaps in expertise, demographics, and lived experiences that may be missing from the board. For example, if the matrix reveals a lack of financial expertise or underrepresentation of certain demographic groups, the committee can prioritize recruitment in these areas.

Once gaps are identified, the Governance Committee takes a proactive approach to recruit potential board members. This includes targeted outreach through community networks, nonprofit leadership programs, and industry connections. Prospective members may be invited to informational sessions or "board preview" meetings to learn more about the role and expectations. This intentional recruitment strategy ensures that new members bring fresh perspectives and essential skills that align with the organization's strategic goals.

In addition to recruitment, the Governance Committee also reviews and refines the overall structure of the board. This includes ensuring that essential leadership roles, such as Chair, Vice Chair, Secretary, and Treasurer, are filled by qualified and committed individuals. The committee may facilitate succession planning by identifying potential future leaders within the board and ensuring they have the development and support needed to transition into these roles. This process strengthens leadership continuity and maintains the stability of the board's governance structure.

Recruitment, Onboarding, and Offboarding of Board Members

The Governance Committee oversees the entire life cycle of a board member's tenure, from recruitment to onboarding to offboarding. Each stage of this cycle is critical to maintaining a strong and effective board.

Recruitment begins with identifying the skills, experiences, and perspectives that the board needs to achieve its strategic goals. This process often involves using a board recruitment matrix to visualize gaps in skills and diversity. The committee develops a targeted recruitment plan, which includes outreach through professional networks, industry events, and community partners. Prospective board members may be invited to informational sessions or "board previews" to learn more about the role. Candidates typically submit an application, followed by an interview process conducted by Governance Committee members. The committee then presents final candidates to the full board for approval.

Onboarding is a structured process designed to integrate new board members quickly and effectively. The onboarding experience begins once a new member is approved by the board. The committee ensures new members receive an orientation packet, which includes governance policies, financial reports, and strategic planning documents. New members also participate in orientation sessions, where they meet key staff, learn about the organization's mission, and become familiar with their roles and responsibilities. Mentorship programs may be offered, pairing new members with experienced board members to facilitate learning and relationship-building.

Offboarding occurs when a board member's term ends or they resign early. The Governance Committee ensures a smooth transition by facilitating a formal departure process. This process may include conducting an exit interview to gather feedback on the board member's experience and insights on how the board can improve. Any unresolved issues, such as returning organizational materials or completing outstanding commitments, are addressed during offboarding. This process provides an opportunity for reflection and continuous improvement, as the committee can incorporate feedback into future recruitment and onboarding strategies.

Annual Timeline and Key Milestones

An effective Governance Committee follows an annual timeline to ensure key responsibilities are addressed throughout the year. By scheduling critical activities each quarter, the committee maintains a proactive approach to board development.

Quarterly Activities and Deadlines

- **Quarter 1 (July - September)**: Review and update board composition and structure. Identify term expirations and prepare recruitment plans.

- **Quarter 2 (October - December)**: Begin active recruitment of new board members. Update onboarding materials and plan for board member evaluations.

- **Quarter 3 (January - March)**: Conduct board member self-assessments and full board evaluations. Review the effectiveness of board roles and responsibilities.

- **Quarter 4 (April - June)**: Finalize onboarding plans for new members. Ensure seamless leadership transitions and support board officer elections.

Timeline for Recruiting and Onboarding New Members

Recruiting and onboarding new board members requires intentional planning. Here's a recommended timeline:

1. **Months 1-2**: Identify skills gaps and diversity needs using the board recruitment matrix. Begin outreach and networking to source potential candidates.

2. **Months 3-4**: Conduct interviews with prospective members. Use a formal application process to ensure transparency and accountability.

3. **Month 5**: Present candidate recommendations to the full board for approval.

4. **Month 6**: Onboard new members, including orientation sessions, introductions to the executive leadership team, and training on governance practices.

Tools for Success

Governance Committee members have access to several tools that support effective recruitment, onboarding, and board development.

Board Recruitment Matrix / Diversity Matrix

The Board Recruitment Matrix is a tool used to visualize the current composition of the board. It maps each member's skills, demographics, and lived experiences, helping the Governance Committee identify gaps and target recruitment efforts. By comparing the board's current strengths to its strategic needs, the committee can prioritize recruitment of individuals who fill specific roles, skills, or demographic needs.

Orientation Packets and Onboarding Guides

Orientation packets provide essential information for new board members. These packets typically include:

- Board member job descriptions

- Governance policies and procedures

- Meeting schedules and agendas

- Financial reports and the organization's latest strategic plan

- Contact information for key staff and other board members

The onboarding process is an opportunity to build engagement and excitement. A clear onboarding guide walks new members through their first 90 days, ensuring they feel confident and connected to the organization's mission.

Board Member Self-Assessments and Board Evaluations

Self-assessments and board evaluations are critical tools for continuous improvement. The Governance Committee coordinates self-assessments, where board members reflect on their contributions, skills, and participation. Full board evaluations assess the board's overall effectiveness, identifying areas where governance processes, participation, or engagement could improve. These tools promote accountability, growth, and ongoing development.

Meeting Structure and Facilitation

Governance Committee meetings should be well-structured, with a clear agenda, action items, and opportunities for reflection. Effective facilitation ensures the committee remains focused on strategic priorities rather than day-to-day operational issues. The Committee Chair is typically responsible for facilitating these meetings, as they have a deep understanding of the committee's objectives and are best positioned to keep discussions on track. The Chair's role includes guiding the agenda, encouraging participation from all members, and ensuring that key decisions are documented and follow-up actions are clearly assigned. If the Chair is unavailable, the Vice Chair or another designated committee member may step into the facilitator role.

Key Discussion Topics for Governance Committee Meetings

- Board composition review and recruitment planning

- Review of board member applications and interview outcomes

- Evaluation of board member performance and overall board effectiveness

- Planning for upcoming board transitions, including leadership elections
- Review of governance policies and recommendations for updates

Best Practices for Agenda Setting and Time Management

- **Agenda Setting**: Draft the agenda in advance, focusing on strategic priorities. Include clear objectives for each agenda item, and share the agenda with committee members prior to the meeting.

- **Time Management**: Use a time-bound agenda that allocates specific durations for each topic. Ensure there is sufficient time for meaningful discussion of key issues.

- **Facilitation**: The committee chair should keep discussions on track, ensure all voices are heard, and clearly define next steps for follow-up action items.

Sample Governance Committee Meeting Agenda

Date: [Insert Date]
Time: [Insert Time]
Location: [Insert Location or Virtual Link]

1. **Welcome and Call to Order** (5 minutes)

   o Chair's welcome and meeting objectives

- o Roll call and introduction of new members (if applicable)

2. **Consent Agenda** (10 minutes)

   - o Approval of previous meeting minutes

   - o Review of routine updates and reports

3. **Board Composition and Recruitment** (20 minutes)

   - o Review board composition using the board recruitment matrix

   - o Identify gaps in skills, demographics, or lived experiences

   - o Update on recruitment progress and candidate outreach

4. **Onboarding and Orientation** (15 minutes)

   - o Review onboarding plans for new members

   - o Update on orientation packet revisions and training schedule

   - o Discussion of mentor assignments for new board members

5. **Board Evaluations and Self-Assessments** (20 minutes)

   - o Review results of board member self-assessments

- Discuss findings and areas for improvement

- Plan for follow-up actions based on evaluation results

6. **Governance Policies and Procedures** (15 minutes)

    - Review existing governance policies for updates or revisions

    - Discuss proposed changes and prepare for full board presentation

7. **Action Items and Next Steps** (10 minutes)

    - Recap of key decisions made during the meeting

    - Assignment of follow-up tasks and deadlines

    - Confirm date and time of the next committee meeting

8. **New Business and Open Floor** (10 minutes)

    - Opportunity for committee members to raise additional topics

9. **Adjournment**

    - Chair closes the meeting and confirms next steps

This agenda format provides a structured approach to Governance Committee meetings, ensuring that all critical topics are addressed and that committee members remain focused on strategic priorities.

Staff Liaison Roles and Responsibilities

The Governance Committee relies on support from staff liaisons to ensure smooth operations and timely follow-up on key activities. Staff play a critical role in managing logistics, facilitating communication, and maintaining governance records.

Who Should Support This Committee?

The Governance Committee is often supported by the following key staff positions:

- **Chief Operating Officer (COO)**: The COO serves as a key liaison between the Governance Committee and the executive leadership team. They provide administrative support, help prepare recruitment materials, and ensure board policies are updated.

- **Board Liaison or Governance Specialist**: This role supports the committee by managing documentation, coordinating meeting schedules, and preparing governance reports. They often handle the onboarding process for new board members.

Role of the Chief Operating Officer, Board Liaison, or Governance Specialist

- **Chief Operating Officer (COO)**: The COO provides strategic oversight of board governance processes.

They support the committee by offering data on board composition, updating policies, and ensuring all board materials are up to date. The COO may also participate in onboarding new members to help them understand operational procedures and their role as board members.

- **Board Liaison or Governance Specialist**: This staff member ensures that Governance Committee meetings run smoothly. They distribute pre-meeting materials, take meeting minutes, and track action items. The liaison also plays a key role in maintaining the board's recruitment matrix and tracking board member term limits and evaluations.

The Governance Committee is essential to the long-term health and effectiveness of a nonprofit's board. By ensuring the board's composition aligns with strategic needs, facilitating recruitment and onboarding, and leading continuous improvement efforts, the Governance Committee helps build a governance structure that is strong, diverse, and well-prepared for future challenges. With support from staff liaisons and tools like recruitment matrices and self-assessments, the committee can maintain a proactive approach to board development. Ultimately, a well-functioning Governance Committee sets the stage for a board that is strategic, engaged, and ready to fulfill its fiduciary duties.

Chapter 3: The Finance Committee

Role and Purpose of the Finance Committee

The Finance Committee plays a crucial role in safeguarding the financial health of the organization. This committee is responsible for overseeing the organization's financial performance, ensuring transparency and accountability in fiscal management, and supporting long-term financial sustainability. By providing financial oversight, the committee enables the board to make informed decisions that align with the organization's strategic goals.

Oversight of the Organization's Financial Health

The Finance Committee's primary role is to maintain a clear picture of the organization's financial health. Members review and analyze financial statements, monitor cash flow, and assess financial risks. By tracking income, expenses, and overall financial performance, the committee ensures that the organization operates within its means and has the resources needed to achieve its mission. The committee also identifies potential financial risks and develops mitigation strategies to safeguard the organization's stability.

Review and Approval of Budgets, Financial Reports, and Major Expenditures

The Finance Committee works closely with the Chief Financial Officer (CFO) or Director of Finance to develop, review, and recommend the annual operating budget for board approval. This process requires balancing revenue projections with planned expenditures, ensuring that the budget supports the strategic priorities of the organization. The committee also reviews periodic financial reports, such as income statements and balance sheets, to monitor performance against the approved budget. Additionally, any major expenditures, capital investments, or changes to financial policies are brought to the committee for review and recommendation to the full board.

Annual Timeline and Key Milestones

An effective Finance Committee follows an annual timeline to ensure timely review of financial reports, budget planning, and risk assessments. Establishing key milestones for each quarter allows the committee to maintain a proactive approach to financial management.

Budget Development, Mid-Year Review, and Year-End Financials

Quarter 3 (January - March)

- **Launch Annual Budgeting Process**
    - **Responsible Party:** CFO, Department Heads
    - **Start Date:** January 1

- **Notes:** Launch the budgeting process for the upcoming fiscal year. Schedule meetings with department heads to gather input on resource needs. Review revenue forecasts, cost assumptions, and proposed expenditures. Identify financial goals and resource needs for the next fiscal year.

- **Mid-Year Financial Performance Review**

  - **Responsible Party:** CFO, Finance Team

  - **Due Date:** January 31

  - **Notes:** Conduct a review of mid-year financial performance to identify necessary budget adjustments. Provide recommendations to the Board for any budget amendments.

- **Present Draft Budget to Finance Committee**

  - **Responsible Party:** CFO, Finance Committee

  - **Due Date:** March 1

  - **Notes:** Present the draft budget to the Finance Committee for review and refinement. Incorporate any recommended changes prior to submission to the Board.

- **Review and Revise Revenue Projections**

  - **Responsible Party:** CFO, Finance Team

  - **Due Date:** March 31

- Notes: Revisit revenue projections and expenditure assumptions for year-end planning.

Quarter 4 (April - June)

- **Finalize Draft Budget and Present to Full Board**

    - **Responsible Party:** CFO, Finance Committee, Full Board

    - **Due Date:** April 30

    - **Notes:** Finalize the draft budget and present it to the full board for approval. Ensure that all necessary updates from Q3 review are included.

- **Re-submit Revised Budget to Full Board (if necessary)**

    - **Responsible Party:** CFO, Finance Committee, Full Board

    - **Due Date:** April 30

    - **Notes:** Re-submit the revised budget to the full board if significant changes are identified in Q3 review.

- **Finalize Year-End Financial Statements**

    - **Responsible Party:** CFO, Finance Team

    - **Start Date:** June 1

- o **Due Date:** June 30

- o **Notes:** Finalize the year-end financial statements. Ensure all outstanding liabilities are addressed, and prepare for the external audit process.

Starting the budgeting process for the next fiscal year early in the current fiscal year is a strategic decision that allows for thoughtful planning, inclusive participation, and more accurate projections. Launching the process in Quarter 1 (July - September) provides ample time to engage department heads, assess resource needs, and review prior-year performance. This early start enables the organization to identify potential revenue challenges, make necessary adjustments, and avoid rushed decisions later in the year. Additionally, it allows the Finance Committee and board members to review and refine the budget before final approval, ensuring it aligns with the organization's strategic priorities. Early budgeting also provides leadership with greater flexibility to address emerging needs or unexpected shifts in funding, creating a more agile financial strategy.

Timeline for Planning Organizational Goals That Affect the Budget

1. **Quarter 1 (July - September):** Begin discussions on strategic goals for the following fiscal year. Identify key programmatic priorities, potential grant opportunities, and anticipated staffing needs. This stage allows leaders and department heads to

45

assess long-term needs and resource requirements.

2. **Quarter 2 (October - December):** Refine strategic goals based on input from staff, stakeholders, and board members. Align goals with the budget by assigning preliminary cost estimates to each objective. This alignment ensures that financial resources will be available to support key initiatives.

3. **Quarter 3 (January - March):** Finalize organizational goals for the next fiscal year. Goals should be clearly defined, measurable, and tied to specific financial resources. The Finance Committee works with department heads to review goal-related cost projections.

4. **Quarter 4 (April - June):** Conduct a final review of organizational goals alongside the development of the draft budget. Ensure that the goals are financially feasible and that sufficient resources have been allocated to achieve them. Final adjustments are made before the board's budget approval process.

Why Planning Goals for the Next Year is Important to the Budget Planning Process

Planning organizational goals for the upcoming fiscal year is essential to the budget planning process because it establishes a clear link between strategy and financial resources. Goals define the organization's priorities, and the budget provides the financial roadmap to achieve those priorities. Without this alignment, the budget may be reactive rather than strategic, leading to resource misallocation or missed opportunities.

By planning goals early, the organization can anticipate funding needs, secure grant funding, and allocate resources to the most impactful initiatives. It also allows for more accurate cost projections and prevents the organization from being caught off guard by unexpected expenses. Moreover, having clear goals in place enables the Finance Committee to create a more focused, mission-driven budget that supports long-term growth and impact. This intentional approach strengthens the organization's financial health and increases accountability to donors, funders, and stakeholders.

Tools for Success

Finance Committees rely on several key tools to fulfill their responsibilities. These tools ensure transparency, improve decision-making, and provide a clear view of the organization's financial position.

Budget Templates, Financial Dashboards, and Variance Reports

- **Budget Templates**: A standardized budget template allows for consistent input of revenue and expense projections. This tool enables the Finance Committee to assess proposed budgets, review cost assumptions, and identify areas for adjustment.

- **Financial Dashboards**: Dashboards provide a visual summary of key financial metrics, such as cash flow, revenue, and expenses. These real-time visuals offer a clear snapshot of financial health, allowing the committee to spot trends or warning signs early.

Types of Financial Reports Used by a Nonprofit

1. **Statement of Activities (Profit and Loss Statement)**: This report shows the organization's revenue, expenses, and net income over a specific period. It provides insight into the nonprofit's operational performance and highlights whether the organization is operating at a surplus or deficit. This report is crucial for tracking financial sustainability, identifying areas of overspending, and making decisions about cost control or revenue generation.

2. **Balance Sheet (Statement of Financial Position)**: The balance sheet outlines the organization's assets, liabilities, and net assets at a specific point in time. It provides a snapshot of the organization's financial stability and liquidity. This report is essential for assessing the financial health of the nonprofit and determining whether it has the resources to meet its obligations and pursue strategic initiatives.

3. **Cash Flow Statement**: This report tracks the flow of cash in and out of the organization over a period of time. It shows how operating, investing, and

financing activities impact cash balances. Understanding cash flow is critical for liquidity management, as it ensures the nonprofit has enough cash on hand to meet immediate financial obligations, such as payroll and vendor payments.

4. **Budget vs. Actual Report**: This report compares the organization's actual financial performance to the budgeted amounts. It highlights variances in revenue and expenses, enabling the Finance Committee to analyze deviations from the plan. This report supports accountability and allows for timely course corrections in spending or revenue generation.

5. **Grant Reporting**: Many funders require detailed financial reporting to ensure grant funds are being used in accordance with grant terms. These reports often include a summary of how funds were spent, any variances from the original grant budget, and progress toward program goals. Grant reports are essential for maintaining funder trust and ensuring continued funding.

6. **Internal Management Reports**: These customized reports provide key financial information tailored to the needs of executive leadership or board members. Examples include financial dashboards, KPI reports, and ad hoc financial analyses. Internal management reports support real-time decision-making and ensure that leadership has access to timely and relevant financial information.

Why These Reports Are Important

- **Transparency and Accountability**: Financial reports provide transparency to stakeholders, including board members, funders, and donors. These reports demonstrate how funds are being used and ensure accountability for financial decisions.

- **Informed Decision-Making**: By having access to real-time financial information, the Finance Committee and executive leadership can make more informed, data-driven decisions.

- **Regulatory Compliance**: Nonprofits are required to submit financial reports as part of regulatory filings, such as IRS Form 990. Accurate reports ensure compliance with federal, state, and grant-related requirements.

- **Performance Assessment**: Reports like the Budget vs. Actual and Cash Flow Statement help assess how well the organization is adhering to its financial plan and whether adjustments are needed.

- **Risk Management**: Regular review of financial statements allows the organization to identify financial risks, such as cash flow shortages or increased liabilities, and take corrective action before problems escalate.

By leveraging these financial reports, the Finance Committee can maintain a clear understanding of the organization's financial position, support strategic decision-making, and ensure the nonprofit's long-term sustainability.

- **Variance Reports**: Variance reports compare actual financial performance against the approved budget, highlighting differences between expected and actual results. These reports enable the committee to identify and address significant variances promptly.

Key Performance Indicators (KPIs) and Financial Ratios

- **KPIs**: Key Performance Indicators (KPIs) help track the organization's financial health. Examples include cash-on-hand, operating reserve ratios, and liquidity ratios.

- **Financial Ratios**: Common financial ratios include the current ratio, debt-to-equity ratio, and program expense ratio. These ratios provide insight into the organization's liquidity, solvency, and operational efficiency.

Meeting Structure and Facilitation

Finance Committee meetings should be structured, time-bound, and focused on high-priority financial matters. To ensure efficiency, meeting agendas are typically set in advance and shared with committee members. The Committee Chair is responsible for facilitating the meeting, as they have a clear understanding of the objectives and priorities for each session. The Chair ensures discussions remain on track, encourages participation from all members, and clearly defines action steps and next steps. If the Chair is unavailable, the Vice Chair or another designated member of the Finance Committee may assume the role of facilitator to ensure the meeting runs smoothly.

Monthly, Quarterly, and Ad Hoc Meeting Schedules

- **Monthly Meetings**: Monthly meetings allow for frequent review of cash flow, financial performance, and any immediate financial issues that require attention.

- **Quarterly Meetings**: Quarterly meetings focus on broader financial health, including budget reviews, risk assessments, and financial forecasting.

- **Ad Hoc Meetings**: These meetings are scheduled as needed to address urgent financial matters, such as major expenditures or unexpected revenue shortfalls.

Key Topics for Discussion by Month or Quarter

- **Monthly**: Review cash flow reports, analyze revenue and expense variances, and discuss any immediate financial needs.

- **Quarterly**: Review quarterly financial statements, conduct financial health assessments, and evaluate financial forecasts.

- **Annually**: Finalize the budget, review year-end financial statements, and prepare for the external audit.

Sample Finance Committee Meeting Agenda

Date: [Insert Date]
Time: [Insert Time]
Location: [Insert Location or Virtual Link]

1. **Welcome and Call to Order** (5 minutes)

   o Chair's welcome and overview of meeting objectives

   o Roll call and quorum verification

2. **Consent Agenda** (10 minutes)

   o Approval of previous meeting minutes

   o Review of routine financial reports

3. **Financial Report Review** (20 minutes)

   o Review of income statement (profit and loss)

   o Review of balance sheet (statement of financial position)

   o Cash flow analysis and liquidity update

4. **Budget Discussion** (20 minutes)

   o Updates on budget development process for the upcoming fiscal year

- o Review of budget variances (Budget vs. Actual)
- o Discussion of adjustments or reforecasts needed

5. **Key Financial Decisions** (15 minutes)

   - o Review of pending major expenditures or investments
   - o Approval of any financial policy updates

6. **Audit Preparation and Risk Assessment** (15 minutes)

   - o Update on audit preparation progress
   - o Discussion of key financial risks and mitigation strategies

7. **Action Items and Next Steps** (10 minutes)

   - o Recap of key decisions made during the meeting
   - o Assignment of follow-up tasks and deadlines
   - o Confirmation of date and time for the next committee meeting

8. **New Business and Open Floor** (10 minutes)

   - o Opportunity for committee members to raise additional topics or concerns

9. **Adjournment**

- o   Chair closes the meeting and confirms next steps

Staff Liaison Roles and Responsibilities

The Finance Committee relies on staff support to prepare financial reports, track key deadlines, and ensure compliance with financial policies.

Who Should Support This Committee?

The following staff members typically support the Finance Committee:

- **Chief Financial Officer (CFO) or Director of Finance**: Serves as the primary staff liaison to the committee, providing financial data, preparing reports, and advising on risk and financial strategy.

- **Chief Operating Officer (COO)**: Supports the CFO and Finance Committee by providing operational insights related to staffing, facilities, and technology costs.

Role of the Chief Financial Officer (CFO) or Director of Finance

The CFO or Director of Finance plays a central role in supporting the Finance Committee. Their responsibilities include:

- Preparing financial reports, variance reports, and dashboards for committee review.

- Supporting the development of the annual budget and ensuring alignment with strategic goals.

- Advising the committee on financial risks, liquidity, and key performance indicators (KPIs).

- Assisting with the external audit process and ensuring compliance with accounting standards.

The Finance Committee is a key driver of financial stewardship and accountability within a nonprofit organization. By overseeing financial health, managing budgets, and ensuring transparency, this committee provides the board with the insight needed to make informed financial decisions. With the support of essential tools, staff liaisons, and clearly defined roles, the Finance Committee ensures the organization's long-term financial sustainability.

Chapter 4: The Audit Committee

Role and Purpose of the Audit Committee

The Audit Committee is a critical component of a nonprofit's financial oversight structure. This committee provides an independent review of the organization's financial statements, ensuring transparency, accuracy, and compliance with accounting standards and regulatory requirements. By engaging with external auditors and monitoring the audit process, the Audit Committee helps maintain the integrity of the nonprofit's financial reporting.

Ensuring Independent Review of Financial Statements

One of the Audit Committee's primary responsibilities is to ensure that the organization's financial statements are reviewed independently. This review ensures that financial information is accurate, complete, and free from material misstatements. The committee acts as an independent body that oversees the preparation and presentation of financial statements. This role builds stakeholder trust and provides assurance to funders, donors, and regulators that the nonprofit's financial practices meet accepted accounting standards.

Engaging External Auditors and Reviewing Audit Results

The Audit Committee is responsible for engaging and selecting an external auditor. This process includes issuing a Request for Proposal (RFP), reviewing auditor qualifications, and selecting a firm with the experience and capacity to perform a high-quality audit. Once the audit is underway, the committee facilitates communication between the auditors and the board, ensuring that the audit process runs smoothly. After the audit, the committee reviews the audit findings, management letter, and any identified issues or recommendations. The committee works with staff to address corrective actions, if necessary.

Annual Timeline and Key Milestones

To maintain a proactive approach to the audit process, the Audit Committee follows an annual timeline that outlines key activities and deadlines. This timeline ensures that the organization is well-prepared for the audit and that all regulatory and funder reporting deadlines are met.

Audit Preparation, Engagement, and Review Schedule

RFP Process for Audit Firms

Timeline: 1 Year Prior to Current Audit Cycle
Activities:

- **Responsible Party:** CFO, Audit Committee

- **Start Date:** July 1 (1 year before current audit cycle)

- **Due Date:** July 31

- **Notes:** Spread RFP activities throughout the year as follows:

- **Q1 (July - September):** Identify qualified audit firms and develop the RFP document.

- **Q2 (October - December):** Issue RFP to audit firms and collect responses.

- **Q3 (January - March):** Evaluate proposals, conduct interviews, and shortlist firms.

- **Q4 (April - June):** Select audit firm and finalize the engagement letter.

Quarter 1 (July - September)

- **Initial Audit Planning Meeting**

  - **Responsible Party:** CFO, Audit Committee, External Auditor

  - **Start Date:** July 1

  - **Due Date:** July 15

  - **Notes:** Schedule planning call with external auditors to align on scope, timeline, and documentation needs.

- **Prepare and Send Pre-Audit Request List**

  - **Responsible Party:** CFO, Finance Team

  - **Start Date:** July 16

  - **Due Date:** July 31

  - **Notes:** Request supporting documents from all relevant departments.

- **Internal Review of Financial Records**

- **Responsible Party:** CFO, Finance Team

- **Start Date:** August 1

- **Due Date:** August 15

- **Notes:** Ensure all reconciliations are complete and accurate prior to submission to auditors.

- **Submission of Pre-Audit Documents to Auditor**

  - **Responsible Party:** CFO

  - **Start Date:** August 16

  - **Due Date:** August 31

  - **Notes:** Upload all requested documentation to the auditor's secure portal.

- **Audit Fieldwork Begins**

  - **Responsible Party:** External Auditor, CFO

  - **Start Date:** September 1

  - **Due Date:** September 15

  - **Notes:** Auditors conduct on-site review of financial records and interviews with key staff.

- **Ongoing Communication with Auditors**

  - **Responsible Party:** CFO, Audit Committee

  - **Start Date:** September 1

- o **Due Date:** September 15

- o **Notes:** Address auditor questions and provide timely responses during fieldwork.

Quarter 2 (October - December)

- **Draft Audit Report Review**

  - o **Responsible Party:** CFO, Audit Committee

  - o **Start Date:** October 1

  - o **Due Date:** October 15

  - o **Notes:** Review initial findings and management letter from auditors.

- **Final Audit Report Issued**

  - o **Responsible Party:** External Auditor

  - o **Start Date:** October 16

  - o **Due Date:** October 31

  - o **Notes:** Ensure accuracy of the final report and prepare for board presentation.

- **Presentation of Audit Results to the Board**

  - o **Responsible Party:** CFO, Audit Committee, External Auditor

  - o **Start Date:** November 1

  - o **Due Date:** November 15

- o **Notes:** Present audit report and management letter to the Board of Directors. Address board questions.

- **Submission of IRS Form 990**

  - o **Responsible Party:** CFO

  - o **Start Date:** November 1

  - o **Due Date:** November 15

  - o **Notes:** Submit Form 990 to the IRS or request an extension if necessary.

Quarter 3 (January - March)

- **Audit Follow-Up Actions**

  - o **Responsible Party:** CFO, Finance Team

  - o **Start Date:** January 1

  - o **Due Date:** January 31

  - o **Notes:** Address any recommendations from the auditors, including corrective actions and process improvements.

- **Compliance Review**

  - o **Responsible Party:** CFO, Compliance Officer

  - o **Start Date:** February 1

  - o **Due Date:** February 28

- Notes: Conduct internal review to ensure compliance with audit recommendations.

Quarter 4 (April - June)

- **Audit Close-Out**

  - **Responsible Party:** CFO, Audit Committee
  - **Start Date:** April 1
  - **Due Date:** April 30
  - **Notes:** Conduct final review of audit file and ensure all follow-up actions are complete.

- **Preparation for Next Audit Cycle**

  - **Responsible Party:** CFO, Finance Team
  - **Start Date:** May 1
  - **Due Date:** June 30
  - **Notes:** Begin initial preparation for the next audit cycle. Identify potential issues and prepare for the RFP process in the next fiscal year.

Key Deadlines for Submission of Reports to Funders/Regulators

- **IRS Form 990**: Typically due 4.5 months after the end of the fiscal year (e.g., November 15 for a fiscal year ending June 30).

- **Grant Reports**: Deadlines for grant reports vary by funder. The Audit Committee should coordinate with the Development Team to ensure timely submission.

- **State Filing Requirements**: Each state may have its own deadlines for charitable registration filings, typically in alignment with Form 990 deadlines.

By following this timeline, the Audit Committee ensures that the audit process is well-organized, deadlines are met, and all required submissions are completed on time. One of the most critical submissions managed by the Audit Committee is the IRS Form 990.

What is the IRS Form 990?

The IRS Form 990 is an annual information return that tax-exempt organizations, including nonprofits, must file with the Internal Revenue Service (IRS). Unlike a traditional tax return that calculates a tax liability, Form 990 provides detailed information about a nonprofit's mission, finances, governance, and operations. The form is made publicly available and is often used by potential funders, donors, and watchdog organizations to assess the nonprofit's accountability and transparency.

Why is Form 990 Important?

1. **Transparency and Accountability**: Since the Form 990 is a public document, it provides donors,

funders, and watchdog organizations with insight into the nonprofit's operations and financial practices. It builds trust with stakeholders by demonstrating how funds are being used to support the mission.

2. **Regulatory Compliance**: Filing Form 990 is a legal requirement for most tax-exempt organizations. Failure to file on time can result in fines, penalties, or even the loss of tax-exempt status.

3. **Internal Review Opportunity**: Preparing the Form 990 gives the organization a chance to review its financial position, highlight its accomplishments, and identify areas for operational improvement.

What Does the Form 990 Include?

- **Mission and Program Descriptions**: A narrative section where nonprofits describe their mission, significant activities, and key accomplishments.

- **Financial Information**: Detailed reporting of revenue, expenses, assets, liabilities, and net assets.

- **Executive Compensation**: Disclosure of compensation for key officers, directors, and highly compensated employees.

- **Governance and Compliance**: Questions related to governance practices, policies, and adherence to legal and regulatory obligations.

When is Form 990 Due?

Form 990 is generally due 4.5 months after the close of the organization's fiscal year. For nonprofits with a fiscal year ending on June 30, the Form 990 is typically due on November 15. Extensions can be requested, but timely filing ensures compliance and avoids penalties.

How Does the Audit Committee Support Form 990 Submission?

The Audit Committee plays an essential role in ensuring the accuracy, completeness, and timeliness of Form 990. The committee reviews the draft Form 990 prepared by the CFO or an external accounting firm, verifies key information, and ensures that any issues raised during the audit are addressed. Once the review is complete, the committee recommends the final Form 990 for submission to the IRS. Their oversight ensures that the nonprofit remains in good standing with regulators and demonstrates its commitment to financial transparency.

Tools for Success

To support the work of the Audit Committee, several tools and resources are essential for successful audit preparation, oversight, and follow-up.

Sample Audit Schedules and Preparation Checklists

- **Audit Schedule Template**: This document provides a timeline of key dates, milestones, and deliverables required for the audit process. It helps the Audit Committee stay on track and monitor progress.

Example Audit Schedule Template

Task/Activity	Responsible Party	Start Date	Due Date	Status	Notes
Initial Audit Planning Meeting	CFO, Audit Committee, External Auditor	July 1	July 15	In Progress	Schedule planning call with external auditors
Prepare and Send Pre-Audit Request List	CFO, Finance Team	July 16	July 31	Not Started	Request supporting documents from all departments
Internal Review of Financial Records	CFO, Finance Team	August 1	August 15	Not Started	Ensure all reconciliations are complete and accurate
Submission of Pre-Audit Documents to Auditor	CFO	August 16	August 31	Not Started	Upload documents to auditor's secure portal
Audit Fieldwork Begins	External Auditor, CFO	September 1	September 15	Not Started	Auditors on-site to review records and conduct interviews
Ongoing Communication with Auditors	CFO, Audit Committee	September 1	September 15	Ongoing	Address auditor questions in real-time
Draft Audit Report Review	CFO, Audit Committee	October 1	October 15	Not Started	Review initial findings and

					management letter
Final Audit Report Issued	External Auditor	October 16	October 31	Not Started	Ensure accuracy of the final report and prepare for board presentation
Presentation of Audit Results to the Board	CFO, Audit Committee, External Auditor	November 1	November 15	Not Started	Present audit report and address any board questions
Submission of IRS Form 990	CFO	November 1	November 15	Not Started	Submit Form 990 to IRS (or request extension if needed)

This schedule outlines each major task, the party responsible, the start and due dates, the status, and any key notes or details for successful completion. It provides clarity and accountability for all key stakeholders involved in the audit process.

- **Audit Preparation Checklist**: This checklist outlines key documentation that must be gathered before the audit begins, such as financial statements, grant agreements, payroll records, and bank reconciliations. It ensures that all essential materials are ready for auditor review.

Example Audit Preparation Checklist

Category	Document/Task	Responsible Party	Status	Due Date	Notes
Financial Statements	Year-end financial statements (Income Statement, Balance Sheet, Cash Flow Statement)	CFO, Finance Team	Not Started	July 15	Finalize all financial statements before submission
Banking	Bank reconciliations for all accounts	CFO, Finance Team	In Progress	July 10	Ensure no outstanding reconciliation issues
Revenue	Grant agreements and funding contracts	Development Team	Not Started	July 20	Ensure grant documentation is complete and accessible
Revenue	Contribution reports (donations, pledges)	Development Team	Not Started	July 25	Reconcile donor system reports with accounting records
Payroll	Payroll registers for the fiscal year	HR, Payroll Vendor	In Progress	July 10	Include year-to-date wages, taxes, and benefits
Compliance	Prior-year IRS Form 990 and State Filings	CFO, Finance Team	Not Started	July 5	Ensure copies of all filings are on hand
Legal	Contracts, leases, and major agreements	Legal Counsel, COO	In Progress	July 20	Gather copies of all active contracts

Fixed Assets	Fixed asset register and depreciation schedule	CFO, Finance Team	Not Started	July 15	Update depreciation schedules for any new purchases
Liabilities	Debt schedules and loan agreements	CFO, Finance Team	Not Started	July 25	Ensure all outstanding debt and payment schedules are documented
Internal Controls	Internal control policies and procedures	CFO, COO	Not Started	July 10	Review and update any changes to internal control policies
Board Governance	Board minutes for the fiscal year	Board Liaison	In Progress	July 15	Ensure board minutes are up-to-date and accessible

This checklist ensures that all essential materials are ready for auditor review and that key stakeholders are accountable for their respective tasks. It also provides a clear timeline for task completion, reducing the likelihood of delays during the audit process.

Compliance Checklists and Documentation Guidelines

- **Compliance Checklist**: This tool helps the Audit Committee ensure that the nonprofit meets compliance obligations, such as IRS filings, grant reporting, and state-level charitable registrations.

- **Documentation Guidelines**: Clear guidelines on how to prepare, organize, and store financial documents make it easier for auditors to access records during the audit process. Organized documentation reduces audit delays and facilitates a smooth review.

These tools ensure the Audit Committee can efficiently support audit readiness, track compliance, and document the results of the audit process.

Meeting Structure and Facilitation

Audit Committee meetings are essential for planning, monitoring, and reviewing audit activities. The frequency and structure of these meetings vary based on the stage of the audit cycle. The Committee Chair typically facilitates these meetings, ensuring discussions remain on track, all voices are heard, and clear action steps are established. The Chair's role includes guiding the agenda, addressing key discussion topics, and ensuring that follow-up tasks are clearly assigned. If the Chair is unavailable, the Vice Chair or another senior member of the committee may facilitate the meeting to maintain continuity and ensure progress on audit-related activities.

Annual vs. Quarterly Meeting Schedule

- **Annual Meetings**: These meetings are held at critical points in the audit cycle, such as at the start of the fiscal year to prepare for the audit, mid-year to review progress, and at year-end to review audit results and corrective actions.

- **Quarterly Meetings**: For larger or more complex organizations, quarterly meetings allow for continuous oversight and progress checks. Regular check-ins help prevent last-minute delays or surprises.

Key Topics for Discussion During the Audit Process

- **Audit Engagement Letter**: Review and approve the engagement letter with the external audit firm.

- **Audit Preparation**: Discuss readiness tasks, internal deadlines, and document collection progress.

- **Audit Fieldwork**: Monitor audit fieldwork progress and address any auditor requests for additional documentation.

- **Audit Findings**: Review the audit report, management letter, and corrective action plan.

- **Regulatory Compliance**: Ensure that all audit-related regulatory filings are submitted on time.

The Committee Chair typically facilitates these meetings, as they have the knowledge and authority to guide the discussion and ensure that key decisions are documented. If the Chair is unavailable, the Vice Chair or another member of the committee may serve as facilitator.

Sample Audit Committee Meeting Agenda

Date: [Insert Date]
Time: [Insert Time]
Location: [Insert Location or Virtual Link]

1. **Welcome and Call to Order** (5 minutes)
    - o Chair's welcome and meeting objectives
    - o Roll call and quorum verification

2. **Consent Agenda** (10 minutes)
    - o Approval of previous meeting minutes
    - o Review of routine reports

3. **Audit Preparation Update** (20 minutes)
    - o Status update on pre-audit readiness tasks
    - o Review of pre-audit document checklist progress
    - o Discussion of key issues or outstanding items

4. **Audit Engagement and Fieldwork** (20 minutes)
    - o Confirmation of audit engagement letter
    - o Review of fieldwork schedule and staff availability
    - o Status of document submission to external auditors

5. **Audit Findings and Review** (25 minutes)
    - o Discussion of preliminary audit findings
    - o Review of management letter and key recommendations
    - o Identification of required corrective actions

6. **Regulatory Compliance and Filing Deadlines** (15 minutes)

    o   Status of IRS Form 990 submission

    o   Review of state registration filings

    o   Update on grant reporting deadlines

7. **Action Items and Next Steps** (10 minutes)

    o   Recap of decisions made during the meeting

    o   Assignment of follow-up tasks and deadlines

    o   Confirmation of date and time for the next committee meeting

8. **New Business and Open Floor** (10 minutes)

    o   Opportunity for committee members to raise additional topics

9. **Adjournment**

    o   Chair closes the meeting and confirms next steps

Staff Liaison Roles and Responsibilities

Staff support plays a critical role in ensuring the success of the Audit Committee. Staff members provide essential documentation, respond to auditor requests, and facilitate communication between the committee and the audit firm.

Role of the CFO, Finance Director, or External Auditor

- **Chief Financial Officer (CFO) or Finance Director**: The CFO or Finance Director serves as the primary liaison between the Audit Committee, staff, and external auditors. They oversee the preparation of financial documents, respond to auditor questions, and coordinate any required corrective actions. The CFO ensures that all compliance obligations related to audit filings are met.

- **External Auditor**: The external auditor's role is to provide an independent assessment of the organization's financial health. They conduct fieldwork, review financial records, and issue an audit report with findings and recommendations. The auditor maintains open communication with the Audit Committee and executive leadership throughout the process.

By defining clear roles for staff liaisons, the Audit Committee can ensure the audit process runs efficiently, with timely responses to auditor requests and effective implementation of corrective actions.

The Audit Committee serves as a vital safeguard for the financial health, accountability, and transparency of the nonprofit organization. By overseeing the audit process, reviewing financial statements, and ensuring compliance with regulatory requirements, this committee provides assurance to stakeholders, funders, and the public.

Equipped with tools such as audit schedules, compliance checklists, and preparation guides, the committee can maintain a proactive approach to financial oversight. Supported by staff liaisons like the CFO and external auditors, the Audit Committee strengthens the organization's credibility, reduces financial risk, and builds trust with funders, donors, and the community.

Chapter 5: The Development Committee

Role and Purpose of the Development Committee

The Development Committee plays a vital role in ensuring the nonprofit's financial sustainability by overseeing fundraising strategy, supporting revenue generation efforts, and leveraging board member engagement. This committee works in partnership with development staff to secure the financial resources necessary to achieve the organization's mission.

Oversight of Fundraising Strategy and Revenue Goals

The Development Committee is responsible for shaping the organization's overall fundraising strategy. This includes setting revenue goals, developing fundraising campaigns, and ensuring alignment with the nonprofit's strategic plan. The committee works with development staff to identify key funding sources, including individual donors, grants, corporate sponsorships, and special events. Regular reviews of fundraising performance allow the committee to assess progress toward revenue targets and adjust strategies as needed.

Board Members' Role in Fundraising

One of the most critical responsibilities of the Development Committee is to ensure board member participation in fundraising. Board members play a key role as ambassadors, advocates, and fundraisers for the organization. The committee encourages all board members to make a financial contribution, support donor engagement, and participate in major fundraising events or campaigns. Board members may also assist in identifying prospective donors and leveraging their personal networks to secure funding.

Diversification in Funding Sources

Diversification of funding sources is a fundamental strategy for ensuring the long-term financial health and sustainability of a nonprofit organization. Relying too heavily on one type of funding, such as a single grant or a major donor, increases financial risk. If that funding source were to end, the organization's operations could be significantly impacted. Diversification spreads this risk by developing multiple revenue streams.

Types of Funding Sources

1. **Individual Donors**: Contributions from individual donors, including major gifts, monthly giving programs, and annual appeals.

2. **Grants**: Funds received from private foundations, corporate foundations, and government agencies. Grant funding often requires applications, reporting, and adherence to specific use requirements.

3. **Corporate Sponsorships**: Partnerships with corporations that provide funding in exchange for

visibility, brand alignment, or community engagement opportunities.

4. **Special Events**: Revenue generated from fundraising events such as galas, auctions, or community-based events.

5. **Earned Income**: Revenue from products, services, or social enterprise ventures run by the nonprofit, such as selling merchandise or offering fee-based services.

6. **Planned Giving and Bequests**: Long-term giving commitments where donors pledge to leave gifts in their wills or estates.

Why Diversification is Important

1. **Financial Stability**: A diversified funding model ensures the organization can continue operations even if one revenue source is reduced or eliminated.

2. **Flexibility and Growth**: Diversification provides the flexibility to fund new initiatives, take advantage of opportunities, and adapt to changes in the external environment.

3. **Reduced Risk**: Relying too heavily on one revenue source (like a single grant) can leave the organization vulnerable. Diversification mitigates this risk.

4. **Increased Credibility**: Diversified revenue demonstrates to funders, donors, and partners that

the organization is stable and well-managed, making it more attractive for future support.

By diversifying its funding streams, a nonprofit positions itself for greater financial health and operational resilience. The Development Committee plays a vital role in building these diversified revenue streams and ensuring the organization's long-term sustainability.

Annual Timeline and Key Milestones

To maintain a proactive approach to fundraising, the Development Committee follows an annual timeline that aligns with key fundraising activities, campaigns, and deadlines. This ensures that the organization remains on track to meet revenue goals.

Key Fundraising Campaigns, Appeals, and Grant Deadlines

- **Quarter 1 (July - September)**: Launch planning for year-end giving campaigns, finalize donor segmentation, and develop appeal strategies. Review grant opportunities and prepare application deadlines.

- **Quarter 2 (October - December)**: Execute year-end giving campaigns, including email appeals, direct mail, and social media fundraising. Focus on donor engagement activities and stewardship of key donors.

- **Quarter 3 (January - March)**: Conduct a "thank you" campaign for year-end donors, assess results of prior campaigns, and evaluate grant success rates. Identify new funding opportunities for the upcoming fiscal year.

- **Quarter 4 (April - June)**: Focus on spring appeals, event planning, and major donor cultivation. Review revenue performance for the year and assess gaps in funding. Prepare a year-end fundraising report for the board.

Seasonal Focus of Fundraising Activities

Different fundraising activities require attention at various points in the year. For example, year-end giving (November-December) is often the most crucial period for donor appeals. In the spring, organizations may focus on fundraising events and donor stewardship activities. During the summer months, the Development Committee may prioritize grant applications, strategic planning, and preparation for fall campaigns.

Tools for Success

The Development Committee relies on various tools to support fundraising initiatives, track progress, and manage donor engagement. These tools streamline processes, ensure accountability, and enhance fundraising performance.

Donor Prospecting Tools, CRM Systems, and Grant Calendars

- **Donor Prospecting Tools**: Platforms like DonorSearch and WealthEngine help identify high-capacity donors and build prospect lists. The committee uses these tools to focus outreach efforts and secure major gifts.

- **CRM Systems**: Customer Relationship Management (CRM) software like Salesforce or Bloomerang tracks donor interactions, contributions, and communications. CRMs enable personalized donor engagement and support targeted appeals.

- **Grant Calendars**: A grant calendar tracks upcoming deadlines for grant proposals, renewal applications, and reporting deadlines. It ensures timely submissions and accountability to funders.

Campaign Planning Templates and Fundraising Checklists

- **Campaign Planning Templates**: Templates guide the planning and execution of fundraising campaigns, including key messages, donor segmentation, and outreach schedules. These templates help the committee track deliverables and assign responsibilities.

- **Fundraising Checklists**: Checklists ensure that no key steps are missed during major campaigns or events. This includes tasks like preparing donor lists, scheduling social media posts, and ensuring thank-you letters are sent on time.

Meeting Structure and Facilitation

Effective Development Committee meetings keep members engaged, focused on fundraising goals, and committed to supporting the nonprofit's mission. Meetings should be time-bound, action-oriented, and well-facilitated.

Ideal Frequency and Timing of Meetings

- **Monthly Meetings**: For large-scale fundraising campaigns or high-urgency deadlines, monthly meetings keep the committee on track.

- **Quarterly Meetings**: A quarterly schedule is appropriate for long-term planning and fundraising strategy updates.

The frequency of meetings depends on the intensity of fundraising activities at any given point in the year. For instance, during year-end giving season, more frequent check-ins may be necessary.

Sample Development Committee Meeting Agenda

Date: [Insert Date]
Time: [Insert Time]
Location: [Insert Location or Virtual Link]

1. **Welcome and Call to Order** (5 minutes)

    o Chair's welcome and review of meeting objectives

    o Roll call and quorum verification

2. **Consent Agenda** (10 minutes)

    o   Approval of previous meeting minutes

    o   Review of campaign progress reports

3. **Fundraising Strategy Review** (20 minutes)

    o   Review of current fundraising campaigns and appeals

    o   Update on major donor outreach and cultivation progress

4. **Donor Engagement and Stewardship** (20 minutes)

    o   Review of key donor stewardship activities

    o   Discussion of board member participation in donor outreach

5. **Grant Opportunities and Proposal Updates** (15 minutes)

    o   Updates on pending grant applications and funding sources

    o   Review of upcoming grant deadlines

6. **Action Items and Next Steps** (10 minutes)

    o   Recap of decisions made during the meeting

    o   Assignment of follow-up tasks and deadlines

- o Confirmation of date and time for the next committee meeting

7. **New Business and Open Floor** (10 minutes)

   - o Opportunity for committee members to raise additional topics

8. **Adjournment**

   - o Chair closes the meeting and confirms next steps

Facilitation Tips

- The Committee Chair or Vice Chair should serve as the primary facilitator. They guide the agenda, encourage participation, and keep discussions focused.

- Assign time limits to agenda items to keep the meeting on schedule.

- Conclude with a clear summary of action items, deadlines, and next steps.

Staff Liaison Roles and Responsibilities

Effective staff support is critical to the Development Committee's success. Staff serve as key facilitators, ensuring the committee has access to data, materials, and resources.

Role of the Chief Development Officer (CDO) or Development Director

The Chief Development Officer (CDO) or Development Director plays a key role in supporting the Development Committee. Their responsibilities include:

- **Campaign Support**: Develops campaign strategies, coordinates donor outreach, and tracks campaign performance.

- **Donor Stewardship**: Assists with donor communications, thank-you letters, and personalized engagement activities.

- **Grant Management**: Oversees grant application processes, tracks deadlines, and coordinates grant reporting requirements.

- **Fundraising Reporting**: Provides regular updates on campaign performance, donor engagement, and progress toward revenue goals.

The Chief Development Officer (CDO) or Development Director serves as a pivotal force behind the Development Committee's efforts, ensuring that board members are fully informed, engaged, and equipped to fulfill their fundraising responsibilities. By providing timely data, strategic insights, and logistical support, the CDO empowers the committee to make informed decisions that directly impact the organization's revenue and sustainability. With the support of the CDO, board members become more effective ambassadors and advocates, engaging donors, cultivating relationships, and expanding the organization's network of supporters.

This collaborative effort results in a mission-driven development strategy that not only sustains current financial needs but also positions the nonprofit for long-term growth. By leveraging board member participation, optimizing fundraising campaigns, and utilizing tools like CRMs and donor prospecting software, the Development Committee creates a diversified and resilient funding base. As a result, the nonprofit becomes better prepared to navigate economic shifts, seize new opportunities, and expand its mission impact. The role of the Development Committee, supported by the CDO, is a clear demonstration of how strategic fundraising efforts drive both financial health and mission success.

Chapter 6: The Program(s) Committee

Role and Purpose of the Program Committee

The Program Committee plays a crucial role in ensuring that a nonprofit's programs are effective, impactful, and aligned with the organization's mission. This committee serves as a bridge between the board's strategic oversight and the operational execution of programs. By evaluating program outcomes, monitoring impact, and ensuring alignment with strategic goals, the Program Committee supports continuous improvement and programmatic excellence.

Oversight of Program Impact, Outcomes, and Alignment with Mission

The Program Committee is responsible for ensuring that all organizational programs are aligned with the nonprofit's mission and strategic priorities. Committee members review program outcomes and impact data to assess whether the programs are meeting their intended goals. By evaluating key performance indicators (KPIs) and assessing program effectiveness, the committee provides recommendations on how to improve programs or reallocate resources to achieve greater mission impact.

Ensuring Programs Align with Strategic Plan

Programs should be closely aligned with the organization's strategic plan. The Program Committee works with program staff to ensure that program objectives support larger organizational goals. This alignment guarantees that resources are being used effectively and that programs are contributing to the organization's long-term success. The committee helps identify any potential gaps or misalignments and recommends adjustments to keep programs focused on the nonprofit's core mission.

Who Should Serve on the Program Committee?

The Program Committee should be composed of individuals who have diverse expertise, a deep understanding of the nonprofit's mission, and a commitment to driving impact. Here's a breakdown of the ideal members to include on this committee:

1. **Board Members**: Board members with experience in program development, evaluation, or specific content expertise related to the nonprofit's mission (e.g., education, health, or social services) bring valuable insights to the committee. They ensure the committee's decisions remain aligned with the strategic priorities of the board.

2. **Program Staff**: Senior program staff, such as Program Directors or Program Managers, should serve as ex-officio members. Their hands-on knowledge of program operations ensures that discussions are grounded in operational realities.

3. **Subject Matter Experts**: External experts with specialized knowledge of the nonprofit's field (e.g.,

educators for education programs, healthcare professionals for health initiatives) provide an external perspective. These experts can offer best practices and innovative ideas to enhance program design and delivery.

4. **Evaluation Specialists**: If the nonprofit has an Evaluation Specialist or Monitoring and Evaluation (M&E) professional on staff, their inclusion on the committee is essential. They provide technical support on data collection, impact measurement, and evaluation methods.

5. **Community Representatives**: Inviting a representative from the community served by the nonprofit's programs adds a critical voice to the committee. Their lived experience provides a firsthand perspective on how the programs are perceived and their actual impact.

6. **Grant and Compliance Staff**: If grant reporting and compliance are a major component of the nonprofit's work, it's beneficial to include the Grant Manager or Compliance Officer. Their role is to ensure that the program's activities align with funder requirements and reporting deadlines.

By incorporating this diverse group of individuals, the Program Committee is better equipped to provide oversight, ensure mission alignment, and strengthen the organization's ability to achieve programmatic success.

Annual Timeline and Key Milestones

An annual timeline provides structure to the work of the Program Committee. Key deadlines related to evaluations, reporting, and grant compliance ensure the organization stays on track and meets its obligations to funders, stakeholders, and beneficiaries.

Evaluation, Program Review, and Reporting Deadlines

- **Quarter 1 (July - September):** Launch program evaluations for the previous fiscal year. Begin planning for any new programmatic initiatives outlined in the strategic plan.

- **Quarter 2 (October - December):** Conduct mid-year program reviews. Track program outcomes and progress toward goals. Review grant deliverables and prepare for any required reporting.

- **Quarter 3 (January - March):** Review findings from mid-year program evaluations. Address any challenges or roadblocks identified. Finalize the annual program evaluation process.

- **Quarter 4 (April - June):** Prepare and submit final program reports for funders and stakeholders. Close out grant reporting deadlines and ensure all obligations are met.

Key Grant/Contract Reporting Dates

- **Monthly or Quarterly Reports:** Many grants require monthly or quarterly progress reports. The committee ensures these reports are submitted on time.

- **Annual Reports**: Many funders request an annual summary of program performance. The committee supports the development of these reports and ensures they highlight impact and outcomes.

- **Renewal Applications**: Some grant contracts require reapplication or renewal each year. The Program Committee ensures that deadlines for grant renewals are met.

Tools for Success

The Program Committee relies on several key tools to track program effectiveness, measure outcomes, and support ongoing improvement. These tools allow committee members and program staff to collect, analyze, and present data in a meaningful way.

Program Logic Models, Outcome Measurement Tools, and Dashboards

- **Program Logic Models**: Logic models are visual representations of how a program's inputs, activities, outputs, and outcomes are connected. These models provide a clear framework for evaluating program effectiveness.

Example Program Logic Model

Component	Description	Example

Inputs	Resources required to support the program	Staff, funding, technology, facilities, partnerships
Activities	Actions taken to implement the program	Delivering workshops, conducting training, developing educational materials
Outputs	Direct products or deliverables of activities	Number of participants trained, number of workshops held, materials distributed
Short-Term Outcomes	Immediate changes or benefits for participants	Increased knowledge, enhanced skills, improved confidence
Intermediate Outcomes	Changes that occur after initial outcomes	Behavior change, application of new skills in daily life
Long-Term Outcomes	The broader impact on the community or society	Reduction in poverty, increase in employment, community well-being

This example logic model provides a structured way to understand how a program's resources, actions, and results are interconnected. It allows the Program

Committee to assess where adjustments are needed to achieve desired outcomes and track the overall impact of the program.

- **Outcome Measurement Tools**: Tools like surveys, focus groups, and case studies are used to track and assess program outcomes. These tools help quantify and qualify the impact of specific programs.

- **Dashboards**: Dashboards provide real-time visual updates on key performance metrics. The Program Committee uses dashboards to review progress toward goals and make data-driven decisions.

Difference Between Qualitative and Quantitative Data

- **Quantitative Data**: This refers to numerical data that can be counted, measured, and analyzed statistically. Examples include survey responses, attendance counts, and financial figures. Quantitative data is used to track key performance indicators (KPIs), measure program outputs, and demonstrate measurable results to funders and stakeholders.

- **Qualitative Data**: This refers to descriptive, non-numerical data that provides insight into the experiences, opinions, and perspectives of program participants. Examples include participant testimonials, focus group feedback, and case studies. Qualitative data helps explain the "why" behind the numbers, providing rich context that can inform program improvement and storytelling.

Both qualitative and quantitative data are essential for outcome measurement. Quantitative data demonstrates the scale and measurable impact of a program, while qualitative data provides deeper insight into participant experiences and the intangible benefits of the program.

Surveys, Data Collection, and Reporting Templates

- **Surveys**: Used to collect feedback from program participants, stakeholders, and beneficiaries. Surveys provide direct insights into program satisfaction, effectiveness, and impact.

- **Data Collection Tools**: Spreadsheets, databases, and online platforms (like Google Forms or SurveyMonkey) are used to gather quantitative and qualitative data from program activities.

- **Reporting Templates**: Standardized templates ensure consistent reporting to funders and stakeholders. Templates provide a clear structure for presenting program results, impact, and lessons learned.

Meeting Structure and Facilitation

The Program Committee's meetings provide an opportunity to review program progress, discuss outcomes, and make strategic decisions. Meetings should be well-structured, action-oriented, and focused on supporting continuous improvement.

Ideal Meeting Frequency and Agendas

- **Quarterly Meetings**: Quarterly meetings allow the committee to review progress, monitor performance metrics, and make data-driven decisions.

- **Ad Hoc Meetings**: If an urgent issue arises, such as a grant compliance issue or a major shift in program strategy, ad hoc meetings can be scheduled as needed.

Sample Program Committee Meeting Agenda

Date: [Insert Date]
Time: [Insert Time]
Location: [Insert Location or Virtual Link]

1. **Welcome and Call to Order** (5 minutes)

   o Chair's welcome and review of meeting objectives

   o Roll call and quorum verification

2. **Consent Agenda** (10 minutes)

   o Approval of previous meeting minutes

   o Review of routine program reports

3. **Program Review and Evaluation** (20 minutes)

   o Updates on ongoing program evaluations

o Discussion of preliminary evaluation results

o Review of action steps to improve program outcomes

4. **Grant Reporting and Compliance** (20 minutes)

o Review of grant deliverables and reporting deadlines

o Updates on grant submission status and renewal timelines

5. **Program Improvement and Innovations** (20 minutes)

o Discussion of new program ideas or potential pilot programs

o Review of stakeholder feedback and survey results

6. **Action Items and Next Steps** (10 minutes)

o Recap of key decisions made during the meeting

o Assignment of follow-up tasks and deadlines

o Confirmation of date and time for the next committee meeting

7. **New Business and Open Floor** (10 minutes)

o Opportunity for committee members to raise additional topics

8. **Adjournment**

   ○ Chair closes the meeting and confirms next steps

Staff Liaison Roles and Responsibilities

The Program Committee relies on staff support to manage the data, evaluations, and reports needed for effective oversight. Staff members play a crucial role in ensuring the committee's success.

Role of Program Directors, Grant Managers, and Evaluation Specialists

- **Program Directors**: Oversee the day-to-day implementation of programs. They provide the committee with reports on program status, successes, and challenges.

- **Grant Managers**: Ensure grant deliverables and reporting deadlines are met. They prepare compliance reports and work with program staff to ensure alignment with funder requirements.

- **Evaluation Specialists**: Lead program evaluations and outcome assessments. They design data collection tools, analyze results, and present findings to the committee.

The success of a nonprofit's programs depends heavily on the combined efforts of staff, committee members, and stakeholders working in alignment toward a common goal. By supporting the Program Committee, staff members play an essential role in ensuring that programs remain mission-driven, responsive to community needs, and capable of achieving measurable impact. With access to the right data, evaluation tools, and reporting structures, the Program Committee can make informed decisions that drive continuous improvement. This collaborative effort fosters greater accountability, transparency, and responsiveness, ensuring that the nonprofit's programs not only meet but exceed stakeholder expectations. Through this unified approach, the organization is better positioned to deliver transformative programs that advance its mission and create lasting community impact.

Chapter 7: The Executive Committee

Role and Purpose of the Executive Committee

The Executive Committee plays a vital role in supporting the board's ability to lead, govern, and make timely decisions. This committee serves as an extension of the board and has the authority to act on behalf of the full board between regularly scheduled meetings. The Executive Committee addresses urgent matters, facilitates executive leadership reviews, and ensures smooth succession planning for key leadership roles.

Acting on Behalf of the Full Board Between Meetings

The Executive Committee is empowered to make decisions on behalf of the full board when immediate action is required. This authority allows for agile decision-making on urgent matters such as contract approvals, legal issues, or personnel matters. However, its decision-making power should be clearly defined in the organization's bylaws to prevent overreach. Typically, any decisions made by the Executive Committee are reported to the full board at the next meeting for review and ratification.

Facilitating CEO Performance Reviews and Succession Planning

One of the Executive Committee's most critical responsibilities is facilitating the annual performance review of the CEO/Executive Director. This process includes setting performance goals, collecting feedback from board members, staff, and other key stakeholders through a comprehensive 360-degree review process. This approach provides a well-rounded perspective on the CEO's leadership, decision-making, and organizational impact. The Executive Committee ensures transparency and accountability in the CEO's performance assessment, offering a balanced view of the CEO's strengths and areas for development.

Additionally, the committee oversees succession planning, ensuring a clear plan is in place for temporary or permanent leadership transitions. This includes identifying potential internal candidates, preparing contingency plans for unexpected vacancies, and documenting the process in a formal succession plan. For guidance on succession planning, organizations can reference the templates and resources found in my book, *Policies and Procedures for Nonprofit Success: A Comprehensive Guide to Ethical and Effective Governance.* This book serves as a comprehensive resource, offering step-by-step instructions for developing a succession plan, practical templates, and expert insights on ensuring a smooth transition of leadership. which includes step-by-step instructions for developing a comprehensive succession plan. This proactive approach ensures the organization is prepared for leadership changes, reducing disruptions and maintaining operational stability.

Annual Timeline and Key Milestones

An effective Executive Committee follows a clear timeline of activities and decision-making points to maintain consistency and accountability throughout the year. The Chair of the Executive Committee should be a board member who demonstrates strong leadership, organizational insight, and a deep understanding of the nonprofit's mission and strategic priorities. Typically, the Chair is the Board Chair or President, as this role naturally aligns with their broader governance responsibilities. However, some organizations may select a Vice Chair or a senior board member with governance experience to ensure a dedicated focus on executive matters. The Chair is responsible for facilitating meetings, guiding the CEO's review process, and ensuring that key decisions are communicated to the full board.

Frequency of Meetings and Critical Decision-Making Points

- **Monthly or As-Needed Meetings**: The Executive Committee typically meets monthly to stay informed and address time-sensitive issues. If urgent decisions are required, the committee may convene additional ad hoc meetings.

- **Quarterly Strategic Check-Ins**: Quarterly strategy sessions allow the Executive Committee to review organizational performance, monitor financial health, and assess risk factors.

- **Annual CEO/Executive Director Review**: The Executive Committee ensures that the CEO's review process is initiated and completed on time.

This process typically begins 2-3 months before the end of the fiscal year. The Chair of the Executive Committee should facilitate this process, as they are best positioned to guide discussions, ensure confidentiality, and maintain accountability. The Chair may be supported by other committee members or the Executive Assistant, but ultimate responsibility for facilitation rests with the Chair.

Deadlines for CEO/Executive Director Reviews

- **Preparation (2-3 months before fiscal year-end):** Set review criteria, develop evaluation tools, and collect board feedback.

- **Review (1 month before fiscal year-end):** Conduct the CEO's review meeting, discuss performance feedback, and develop performance goals for the following year.

- **Follow-Up (End of fiscal year):** Finalize performance feedback and adjust the CEO's goals as needed. Share the results of the review with the full board.

Tools for Success

The Executive Committee utilizes specific tools to improve decision-making, support leadership development, and ensure accountability. These tools enable the committee to track progress, facilitate performance reviews, and maintain readiness for leadership transitions.

Executive Dashboard for Key Metrics

- **Purpose**: The dashboard provides a real-time overview of critical organizational metrics, such as financial health, program impact, and operational performance.

- **Key Metrics**: Revenue, expenses, cash flow, strategic goal progress, risk assessments, and human resources metrics.

- **Benefits**: Provides visibility into the organization's overall health and supports data-driven decision-making.

Sample CEO Evaluation Forms and Succession Planning Templates

- **CEO Evaluation Forms**: These forms standardize the CEO review process and allow for input from multiple stakeholders. Evaluation criteria may include leadership, strategic alignment, financial stewardship, and staff engagement.

Sample 360-Degree CEO Evaluation Template

Evaluation Category	Key Questions	Rating Scale (1-5)	Comments/Examples
Leadership	How effectively does the CEO inspire and motivate staff, board members, and stakeholders?	☐1 ☐2 ☐3 ☐4 ☐5	[Provide examples or context]

Strategic Thinking	Does the CEO demonstrate strategic foresight and align operations with the organization's long-term goals?	□ 1 □ 2 □ 3 □ 4 □ 5	[Provide examples or context]
Financial Stewardship	How well does the CEO manage financial resources and ensure fiscal responsibility?	□ 1 □ 2 □ 3 □ 4 □ 5	[Provide examples or context]
Decision-Making	Does the CEO make timely, effective, and well-informed decisions?	□ 1 □ 2 □ 3 □ 4 □ 5	[Provide examples or context]
Communication	Is the CEO an effective communicator with internal and external stakeholders?	□ 1 □ 2 □ 3 □ 4 □ 5	[Provide examples or context]
Stakeholder Engagement	Does the CEO build strong relationships with funders, partners, and community members?	□ 1 □ 2 □ 3 □ 4 □ 5	[Provide examples or context]
Adaptability	How well does the CEO handle change,	□ 1 □ 2 □ 3 □ 4 □ 5	[Provide examples or context]

	uncertainty, or crisis situations?		
Organizational Culture	Does the CEO foster a culture of equity, inclusion, and continuous improvement?	☐ 1 ☐ 2 ☐ 3 ☐ 4 ☐ 5	[Provide examples or context]

Instructions for Use:

1. Each stakeholder (board member, senior staff, key partners) completes the form independently.

2. The Executive Committee collects and aggregates the results, ensuring confidentiality.

3. Comments and examples provided in the "Comments/Examples" column should highlight specific instances that illustrate the CEO's strengths or areas for growth.

4. Results are used to guide the CEO's annual review discussion and inform goal-setting for the next fiscal year.

- **Succession Planning Templates**: These templates outline the steps to identify, train, and prepare internal candidates for key leadership roles. Templates also detail emergency response procedures for sudden leadership transitions.

Meeting Structure and Facilitation

Executive Committee meetings are focused, time-sensitive, and decision-oriented. Meetings are structured to ensure that key topics are addressed efficiently and that actionable outcomes are achieved.

Monthly or As-Needed Meetings

- **Monthly Meetings**: Used to address ongoing strategic initiatives, review financial performance, and discuss operational issues that require immediate action.

- **Ad Hoc Meetings**: Called when urgent matters arise that cannot wait until the next scheduled meeting, such as legal issues, personnel matters, or time-sensitive approvals.

Sample Executive Committee Meeting Agenda

Date: [Insert Date]
Time: [Insert Time]
Location: [Insert Location or Virtual Link]

1. **Welcome and Call to Order** (5 minutes)

   o Chair's welcome and review of meeting objectives

   o Roll call and quorum verification

2. **Consent Agenda** (10 minutes)

   o Approval of previous meeting minutes

   o Review of financial dashboard and performance metrics

3. **Strategic Issues** (20 minutes)

    o Review of key operational or strategic risks

    o Discussion of pending board-level decisions

4. **CEO Performance Review and Succession Planning** (20 minutes)

    o Update on CEO review process and progress

    o Discussion of potential leadership transition needs

5. **Action Items and Next Steps** (10 minutes)

    o Recap of key decisions made during the meeting

    o Assignment of follow-up tasks and deadlines

    o Confirmation of date and time for the next committee meeting

6. **New Business and Open Floor** (10 minutes)

    o Opportunity for committee members to raise additional topics

7. **Adjournment**

    o Chair closes the meeting and confirms next steps

Staff Liaison Roles and Responsibilities

Staff support is essential to the effective functioning of the Executive Committee. Staff liaisons help prepare meeting materials, track action items, and provide administrative support.

Role of the Executive Director/CEO and Executive Assistant

- **Executive Director/CEO**: While the CEO is not a member of the Executive Committee, they often attend meetings to provide operational updates, offer strategic insights, and respond to committee questions. The CEO's role is to support the committee's decision-making process and ensure that operational issues are addressed.

- **Executive Assistant**: The Executive Assistant provides essential administrative support, such as scheduling meetings, preparing agendas, recording meeting minutes, and following up on action items. The assistant ensures that the committee's work runs smoothly and that key deadlines are met.

The Executive Committee plays a pivotal role in ensuring effective governance and operational stability for the nonprofit. By drawing on the expertise of its members, the strategic leadership of the CEO, and the administrative support of essential staff, the committee creates a cohesive and efficient decision-making process. This collaborative structure allows the Executive Committee to act swiftly on behalf of the board, address urgent issues, and maintain momentum on critical organizational priorities. Through its role in facilitating executive reviews and succession planning, the committee strengthens the nonprofit's leadership pipeline and ensures that transitions are smooth and strategic. This proactive approach enhances the organization's capacity for sustained impact, enabling it to continue advancing its mission with clarity and confidence.

Chapter 8: Board Tools, Technology, and Resources

Overview of Essential Tools for Board Governance

Effective board governance relies on the use of key tools and technologies that facilitate collaboration, decision-making, and accountability. By utilizing purpose-built platforms and resources, boards can streamline their operations, improve communication, and increase transparency. This chapter outlines the essential tools and resources every nonprofit board should consider to enhance governance practices.

Board Portals, Document Storage, and Collaboration Platforms

Board portals and document storage platforms provide a centralized location for storing, accessing, and sharing key governance materials. These platforms increase efficiency, improve transparency, and ensure that board members have access to the information they need to make informed decisions.

Key Features of Board Portals:

- **Document Storage**: Securely store board materials, including meeting minutes, financial reports, and governance documents.

111

- **Access Control**: Allow role-based access to protect sensitive information and maintain confidentiality.

- **Collaboration Tools**: Enable board members to comment, discuss, and collaborate on shared documents.

- **Notifications and Reminders**: Send alerts for upcoming meetings, document deadlines, and key action items.

Popular Board Portals and Collaboration Platforms:

- **BoardEffect**: Comprehensive platform for managing board documents, calendars, and communications.

- **Diligent Boards**: A widely used platform that offers document storage, voting tools, and collaboration features.

- **Google Workspace or Microsoft 365**: Simple document-sharing solutions with cloud-based storage, document editing, and collaborative tools.

Tools for Virtual Board Meetings

With the rise of remote work, virtual board meetings have become essential for nonprofit governance. Virtual meeting platforms provide the flexibility to convene board members from anywhere, reduce travel costs, and maintain continuity during emergencies.

Popular Tools for Virtual Meetings:

- **Zoom**: Offers video conferencing, screen sharing, breakout rooms, and recording options for board meetings.

- **Microsoft Teams**: An all-in-one collaboration platform with video meetings, chat, and document sharing.

- **Google Meet**: A lightweight, user-friendly platform for video conferencing that integrates with Google Workspace.

Best Practices for Virtual Board Meetings:

- Share agendas, materials, and reports in advance using a board portal or document-sharing platform.

- Use "breakout rooms" to facilitate small group discussions during meetings.

- Assign a dedicated facilitator or moderator to ensure the meeting stays on track and that all voices are heard.

Templates and Checklists

Templates and checklists help standardize processes, ensure compliance, and support continuous improvement. By having pre-built templates available, board members and staff can save time, maintain consistency, and improve efficiency.

Board Self-Assessments, Skills Matrix, and Diversity Matrix Templates

Board Self-Assessments: Self-assessment tools enable board members to reflect on their performance, identify areas for growth, and strengthen the overall effectiveness of the board.

Skills Matrix: A skills matrix highlights the collective strengths and skills of board members, helping identify gaps in expertise that should be filled during recruitment.

Diversity Matrix: A diversity matrix tracks board member demographics, such as race, gender, age, and lived experience, ensuring that the board reflects the community it serves.

Example Skills Matrix Template

Board Member	Finance/Accounting	Legal	Fundraising	HR	Program Expertise	Diversity Lived Experience
Member 1	☑		☑		☑	☑
Member 2		☑		☑		☑
Member 3	☑		☑	☑		☑

By using these tools, the board can ensure it has the right combination of skills, perspectives, and lived experiences to govern effectively.

Sample Agendas, Minutes, and Facilitation Tools

Agendas: Standardized meeting agendas provide structure, ensure key topics are addressed, and keep meetings on track. Agendas typically include a welcome, approval of prior meeting minutes, key discussion items, financial updates, and action items.

Minutes: Meeting minutes document key decisions, actions taken, and next steps. Accurate minutes serve as a historical record for the board and demonstrate transparency and accountability to funders and regulators.

Facilitation Tools: Effective facilitation ensures that board meetings run smoothly, engage all participants, and result in clear, actionable decisions. Tools to support facilitation include virtual whiteboards (like Miro or MURAL), time trackers, and online polling tools to gauge consensus.

Sample Board Meeting Agenda Template

Date: [Insert Date]
Time: [Insert Time]
Location: [Insert Location or Virtual Link]

1. **Welcome and Call to Order** (5 minutes)

2. **Approval of Agenda and Minutes** (5 minutes)

3. **Executive Director's Report** (20 minutes)

4. **Finance Committee Report** (15 minutes)

5. **Governance Committee Report** (15 minutes)

6. **Program/Impact Report** (15 minutes)

7. **Strategic Discussion** (30 minutes)

8. **Action Items and Next Steps** (10 minutes)

9. **Adjournment**

Tools for Monitoring Bylaws, Policies, and Procedures

Monitoring bylaws, policies, and procedures ensures that the board operates in accordance with legal, ethical, and regulatory standards. Keeping track of these documents requires tools that allow for version control, tracking changes, and ensuring accessibility to all board members.

Tools for Monitoring Bylaws, Policies, and Procedures:

- **Document Management Software**: Tools like Google Drive, Microsoft SharePoint, and Dropbox ensure centralized, cloud-based access to all essential governance documents.

- **Policy Tracking Software**: Platforms like PowerDMS enable organizations to track policy updates, maintain version control, and ensure compliance with regulatory requirements.

- **Bylaw Review Checklists**: Checklists outline the key areas to review when updating bylaws, including voting procedures, officer roles, and board composition.

Example Bylaw Review Checklist

Section	Review Date	Last Revision Date	Status	Notes

Voting Procedures	[Insert Date]	[Insert Date]	Needs Review	Ensure alignment with state law
Officer Roles	[Insert Date]	[Insert Date]	Up-to-Date	No changes needed
Board Composition	[Insert Date]	[Insert Date]	Under Review	Considering a diversity goal
Conflict of Interest	[Insert Date]	[Insert Date]	Needs Review	Clarify disclosure process

Having these tools readily available allows boards to operate more efficiently, remain compliant with regulatory standards, and maintain good governance practices.

The right combination of tools, templates, and resources enables nonprofit boards to operate with efficiency, transparency, and accountability. By investing in technology and tools designed for board governance, nonprofits can ensure smoother collaboration, enhanced oversight, and stronger decision-making. From board portals to skills matrices, these resources support a modern approach to governance, ensuring that boards are well-equipped to meet the challenges of today's nonprofit landscape.

Chapter 9: Conclusion

Final Thoughts on Building a Strong and Effective Board

Building a strong and effective nonprofit board requires a thoughtful approach to governance, leadership, and collaboration. Each committee, from the Board Governance Committee to the Executive Committee, plays a critical role in ensuring that the board operates with clarity, transparency, and purpose. An effective board does not happen by accident—it is intentionally designed, continuously nurtured, and strategically developed over time.

A strong board is one that not only meets its legal and fiduciary responsibilities but also serves as a thought partner for the organization's leadership. It ensures alignment between strategy and operations, supports the CEO or Executive Director, and champions the nonprofit's mission in the broader community. Through the use of effective tools, well-structured committees, and intentional recruitment, nonprofits can create a governance model that is both dynamic and sustainable.

Equally important is the emphasis on board culture. Boards that prioritize equity, inclusion, and belonging foster an environment where diverse perspectives are valued and strategic thinking is strengthened. Such boards are better positioned to address challenges, seize opportunities, and deliver lasting impact.

How to Measure Board Performance and Impact

To ensure continuous improvement, boards must regularly assess their performance and impact. By measuring effectiveness, boards can identify areas for growth, set improvement goals, and strengthen their governance practices. Here are key methods for measuring board performance:

1. Board Self-Assessments

Board self-assessments provide an opportunity for individual board members to reflect on their contributions and for the board as a whole to evaluate its effectiveness. These assessments often include questions on board engagement, strategic oversight, committee performance, and alignment with organizational goals. Self-assessment tools may also ask for feedback on the quality of communication, the clarity of roles and responsibilities, and the effectiveness of board meetings.

2. Skills and Diversity Matrix Reviews

A periodic review of the board's skills and diversity matrix helps ensure that the board maintains a well-rounded composition of skills, lived experiences, and perspectives. By tracking board member expertise in areas such as finance, fundraising, legal, and program oversight, the board can identify gaps in knowledge and recruit new members to fill those gaps.

3. CEO/Executive Director Feedback

Feedback from the CEO or Executive Director provides valuable insights into how well the board is supporting the leadership team. This feedback can identify gaps in board engagement, strategic alignment, or support for key initiatives. It also offers the opportunity to strengthen the relationship between the board and executive leadership.

4. Review of Meeting Effectiveness

Meeting effectiveness can be evaluated using post-meeting surveys or discussions that capture feedback from board members. Questions might focus on whether meetings stayed on track, if agenda items were adequately addressed, and if the board made timely and effective decisions. Improvements in meeting facilitation can lead to more efficient use of board member time.

5. Progress Toward Strategic Goals

Boards are responsible for overseeing the organization's progress toward strategic goals. Reviewing how well the organization is achieving its goals can serve as an indirect measure of board effectiveness. If an organization is consistently meeting its strategic objectives, it's a sign that the board's guidance and oversight are on track.

By incorporating these measurement tools into its governance process, a board can ensure it stays focused, effective, and engaged in advancing the mission of the organization.

Call to Action: Continuous Improvement in Governance

Strong governance is not a one-time achievement—it is an ongoing process of reflection, adaptation, and growth. Just as nonprofit organizations evolve, so too must their boards. Continuous improvement in board governance requires a commitment to learning, feedback, and accountability.

Key Actions for Continuous Improvement:

- **Conduct Annual Self-Assessments**: Ensure that board members and committees reflect on their own performance annually.

- **Use Data to Drive Decisions**: Leverage dashboards, financial reports, and outcome data to make informed governance decisions.

- **Invest in Board Development**: Offer training, workshops, and learning opportunities for board members to strengthen their governance skills.

- **Review and Revise Policies**: Ensure that board policies are up to date, aligned with industry standards, and legally compliant.

As this book has demonstrated, effective nonprofit governance is a dynamic process that requires thoughtful planning, intentionality, and a willingness to adapt. Whether you're a new board member, a committee chair, or an executive leader, your role in building an effective board is critical to the organization's success. By using the frameworks, templates, and tools outlined in this book, your board can move from good to great, ensuring long-term impact and sustainability.

As you continue this journey, remember that excellence in governance is not about perfection—it's about progress. Regularly evaluate, learn from mistakes, and apply those lessons to improve. A strong board is one that remains flexible, mission-focused, and committed to continuous growth.

In closing, I encourage you to take action. Use the tools, templates, and strategies outlined in this book to create a governance model that serves as a model for other nonprofits. Reflect on your board's impact, challenge yourself to strive for excellence, and commit to the ongoing process of growth and learning. By doing so, you'll ensure that your board remains a driving force behind your nonprofit's mission and impact in the community.

Appendix: Board Bylaws Template and Committee Charter Templates

1. Board Bylaws Template

Article I: Name and Purpose

1. **Name**: The name of the organization shall be [Insert Name of Organization].

2. **Purpose**: The organization is organized exclusively for charitable, educational, and community purposes under Section 501(c)(3) of the Internal Revenue Code.

Article II: Membership

1. **Members**: The corporation shall have no members as defined by state law. The Board of Directors shall exercise all corporate powers.

Article III: Board of Directors

1. **General Powers**: The Board of Directors shall manage the affairs of the organization.

2. **Number and Composition**: The Board shall have no fewer than 7 and no more than 15 directors.

3. **Term of Office**: Directors shall serve 3-year terms, renewable for up to 2 consecutive terms.

4. **Meetings**: The Board shall meet at least 4 times per year.

5. **Quorum**: A majority of directors present shall constitute a quorum.

6. **Voting**: Each director shall have one vote, and decisions shall be made by a majority of those present.

7. **Removal**: Directors may be removed by a majority vote of the Board.

8. **Compensation**: Directors shall not receive compensation for their services but may be reimbursed for pre-approved expenses.

Article IV: Officers

1. **Officers**: The officers of the Board shall be Chair, Vice Chair, Secretary, and Treasurer.

2. **Election and Term**: Officers are elected annually by the Board and serve one-year terms.

3. **Duties**:

    o   **Chair**: Presides at all board meetings, facilitates strategic discussions, and serves as the primary liaison to the Executive Director.

- **Vice Chair**: Acts in the absence of the Chair and supports special projects as assigned.

- **Secretary**: Keeps accurate meeting minutes, maintains corporate records, and ensures board compliance with applicable laws.

- **Treasurer**: Oversees financial affairs, monitors financial statements, and reports the organization's financial position to the Board.

Article V: Committees

1. **Standing Committees**: The Board shall maintain the following standing committees:

   - Governance Committee

   - Finance Committee

   - Audit Committee

   - Development Committee

   - Program Committee

   - Executive Committee

2. **Ad Hoc Committees**: The Board may establish ad hoc committees as necessary to address short-term objectives.

3. **Committee Composition**: Committee members shall be appointed by the Board Chair and ratified by the Board.

Article VI: Executive Director

1. **Role**: The Executive Director shall be the chief executive officer of the organization.

2. **Duties**: Responsible for the daily operations of the organization, fundraising, and executing strategic initiatives as directed by the Board.

Article VII: Conflict of Interest

1. **Disclosure**: Board members shall disclose any conflicts of interest annually.

2. **Recusal**: Directors with conflicts shall recuse themselves from relevant discussions and decisions.

Article VIII: Amendments

1. **Amendments**: These bylaws may be amended by a two-thirds vote of the Board after a 30-day notice of proposed changes.

---

2. Committee Charter Templates

Governance Committee Charter

Purpose: To oversee the structure, composition, and effectiveness of the Board.

1. **Responsibilities:**

    o   Develop and implement a comprehensive Board recruitment strategy.

    o   Lead onboarding, orientation, and training of new Board members.

    o   Conduct annual Board evaluations and self-assessments.

    o   Review and recommend changes to Board governance policies.

    o   Ensure diversity, equity, and inclusion are prioritized in Board recruitment and composition.

2. **Membership:** Composed of 3-5 Board members, including the Chair of the Board.

3. **Meetings:** The committee shall meet at least quarterly.

4. **Reporting:** The committee shall report its activities and recommendations to the full Board.

Finance Committee Charter

Purpose: To oversee the organization's financial health, budgets, and internal controls.

1. **Responsibilities:**

   o Oversee the development of the annual budget and recommend it to the Board for approval.

   o Review monthly financial reports and ensure compliance with financial policies.

   o Recommend financial policies and investment strategies to the Board.

   o Review and monitor cash flow, financial statements, and reserve fund balances.

2. **Membership**: Composed of 3-5 Board members, including the Treasurer.

3. **Meetings**: The committee shall meet at least quarterly.

4. **Reporting**: The committee shall report its activities and recommendations to the full Board.

Audit Committee Charter

Purpose: To ensure accuracy, accountability, and transparency in financial reporting.

1. **Responsibilities**:

   - Oversee the selection and engagement of the independent audit firm.

   - Review the independent auditor's findings and monitor corrective actions as needed.

   - Review and approve the organization's IRS Form 990 before submission.

   - Report the audit results and recommendations to the Board.

2. **Membership**: Composed of at least 3 Board members who are not part of the Finance Committee.

3. **Meetings**: The committee shall meet at least twice annually.

4. **Reporting**: The committee shall report its activities and recommendations to the full Board.

Development Committee Charter

Purpose: To support fundraising efforts and ensure financial sustainability.

1. **Responsibilities:**

   o Develop and oversee fundraising plans, including major gifts and annual appeals.

   o Assist in donor cultivation, stewardship, and recognition activities.

   o Track and evaluate the effectiveness of development efforts and recommend adjustments.

   o Collaborate with staff on grant applications and corporate sponsorships.

2. **Membership:** Composed of 3-5 Board members, in addition to relevant staff support as needed.

3. **Meetings:** The committee shall meet at least quarterly.

4. **Reporting:** The committee shall report its activities and recommendations to the full Board.

Program Committee Charter

Purpose: To ensure the alignment of programs with the organization's mission and goals.

1. **Responsibilities**:

   o Monitor and evaluate program effectiveness and impact.

   o Oversee the development of new programs and ensure alignment with strategic priorities.

   o Review and recommend program policies to the Board.

   o Ensure programmatic activities align with grantor requirements.

2. **Membership**: Composed of 3-5 Board members, including program staff as non-voting members.

3. **Meetings**: The committee shall meet at least quarterly.

4. **Reporting**: The committee shall report its activities and recommendations to the full Board.

Executive Committee Charter

Purpose: To act on behalf of the Board on urgent matters between board meetings.

1. **Responsibilities:**

   - Provide oversight of the Executive Director's performance and conduct their annual review.

   - Address urgent issues requiring action between Board meetings.

   - Recommend actions for full Board consideration as needed.

2. **Membership:** Composed of Board officers (Chair, Vice Chair, Secretary, Treasurer) and additional members as deemed necessary.

3. **Meetings:** The committee shall meet as needed.

4. **Reporting:** The committee shall report its activities and recommendations to the full Board.

Recommended Reading

Check out other books from the Nonprofit Success Toolkit Series that can further your knowledge of nonprofit leadership, governance, and operational excellence.

By Matthew B. Scraper

1. *Effective Nonprofit Board Governance: Roles, Responsibilities, and Best Practices for Committees and Directors*

2. *From the Pulpit to the Boardroom: How I Transitioned from a 20-Year Career in Ministry to the Nonprofit Sector*

3. *Policies and Procedures for Nonprofit Success: A Comprehensive Guide to Ethical and Effective Governance*

4. *The Nonprofit Operations Playbook: Understanding Nonprofit Operations for Mission-Driven Organizations*

5. *How to Start a Nonprofit (and Actually Succeed!): A Step-by-Step Guide for Visionaries and Changemakers*

www.ingramcontent.com/pod-product-compliance
Lightning Source LLC
Chambersburg PA
CBHW022002170526
45157CB00003B/1102